PLAN ON LIVING

THE RETIREE'S GUIDE TO LASTING INCOME & ENDURING WEALTH

SCOTT M. PETERSON
Chartered Financial Consultant

ISBN 978-0-9985831-1-2

Printed in the United States of America.

Copy editors: Angela Carter and Emily Davis

Cover and book design: Hales Creative (*halescreative.com*)

Scott M. Peterson is the founder and president of Peterson Wealth Advisors. Peterson Wealth Advisors is a registered investment adviser. Information presented within this book is for educational purposes only and are not intended to be an offer or solicitation for the sale or purchase of any specific securities, investments, or investment strategies. Investments involve risk and, unless otherwise stated, are not guaranteed. Be sure to first consult with a qualified financial adviser and/or tax professional before implementing any strategy discussed herein. Past performance is not indicative of future performance.

ACKNOWLEDGMENTS

Writing a book of this kind takes a lot of time and research. My staff has carried an unusual burden during the last couple of years as they afforded me the time I needed to put this book together. Besides covering my day-to-day responsibilities, my staff was also instrumental in researching the facts and figures that went into this book. I am forever grateful for the professionals I have been able to surround myself with. A special thanks goes to Sarah Bonkosky who, I am sure, is the happiest person to see this book completed. Sarah's patience and expertise have been exceptional.

An additional very special group of people that has made sacrifices so this book could be written is my family. I am likewise thankful for the patience they have demonstrated during the writing of this book. My wife will be getting her husband back and my children will regain their full-time father. I have been forever blessed by marrying my wife, Tracie, and I am thankful for each of my children. Family, your friendship, encouragement, and desire to accomplish great things in your own lives have been an inspiration to me.

CONTENTS

PREFACE

For more than three decades I have had the wonderful opportunity to counsel with hundreds of my retired friends and their families on how to manage their financial affairs through the various stages of retirement. Every day of my career has taught me something new about retirement planning and investing. During this period, I have also learned priceless lessons in human behavior. Guiding euphoric clients through "the best of times" and fearful clients through "the worst of times" has given me valuable insights that no book or classroom can equal.

I originally chose the career path of working with retirees because I knew that, one day, eighty million of my fellow baby boomers would need to tap into my expertise. What I did not foresee was that pension plans, the financial security blanket of previous generations of retirees, would be replaced by 401(k)s and a variety of self-funding retirement savings programs. The shift from pension plans to individually managed accounts transferred the burden of providing a perpetual stream of retirement income from the employer squarely onto the back of the unprepared American worker.

During the course of my career, the topic of retirement income planning became my passion. I am always in search of new and better ways to accumulate, manage, and judiciously distribute retirement resources. As I managed Investments and researched this topic, it became evident that today's retirees are fighting an uphill battle when it comes to securing a reliable income stream throughout retirement. Lacking fundamental investment knowledge, not knowing whom to trust, and being surrounded by confusing and often misleading investment narratives all serve to exacerbate the risks retirees face as they endeavor to succeed in today's high-stakes retirement experiment.

Today's retirees are drowning in information while starving for practical solutions. Therefore, this book is not a technical guide to investing. I do not intend to add to the already burgeoning supply of investment facts and figures that are readily available. Rather, the intent of this book is to help the reader decipher the volumes of information into what is meaningful and what isn't. Armed with this insight, you will have the foundational knowledge of the workings of a retirement income plan. A plan that will be your anchor in the swirling sea of investment volatility and misinformation that will undoubtedly be part of your investment future.

I invite you to join with me on a journey, a journey to secure your financial future. Step back, take a deep breath, and let's get started. Together we can blaze a common-sense path to successfully managing your retirement resources.

INTRODUCTION

The bristlecone pine, the oldest and most durable of all tree species, grows in only a select few high-altitude locations in the western United States. Some of these trees are estimated to be as old as the Egyptian pyramids. Lightning strikes, droughts, temperatures of forty degrees below zero, and snow depths of ten to fifteen feet annually are the challenges of the environment where the bristlecone pine thrives.

If you are retired, or nearing that threshold, you have experienced some extreme financial conditions during your working career that could be likened to the extremes experienced by the bristlecone pine. It should be expected that during your retirement, or the next several decades, financial storms of one kind or another will continue to afflict us with regularity.

The key to a financially successful retirement is to recognize potential risks, and then create a plan that is prepared to withstand whatever comes your way. Sprinkled throughout this book are images of the bristlecone pine, as a reminder that the ultimate goal of an enduring financial plan during retirement is not to avoid every financial storm that comes along—that just can't be done. Rather the goal should be to create a plan that is designed to provide perennial retirement income as well as peace of mind, come what may. Hopefully, as you read this book you will find the information you need to create such a plan. Once this is accomplished, you can plan on living.

Plan on living a full and abundant life. The opportunities facing the baby boomer retirees are endless. Collectively speaking, we have the health, the wealth, and the circumstances afforded to us to accomplish dreams unimaginable to previous generations of retirees. A retirement full of what is most meaningful to you can be your future. Dream big!

Today's retirees need to *plan on living* for a long time. Past generations of explorers sought unsuccessfully to locate the fountain of youth; this generation scrapped the idea of finding this illusive fountain and decided instead to create a fountain of youth of their own. Thus far this endeavor has proven to be remarkably successful. Medical advancements have prolonged life expectancies to the point that many retirees will live into their nineties and beyond. The financial issues surrounding longevity cannot be ignored if retirees are to maintain their financial independence and dignity.

This generation of retirees has an urgency to institute a financial plan *for* living. Keeping our investments ahead of the eroding effects of inflation while avoiding losing money during the occasional stock market downturn is a delicate balancing act. A plan for living three decades without a paycheck requires thoughtful engineering.

Certainly, recessions and temporary stock market declines will be part of our financial future because economies and markets are cyclical. The ideas shared in this book are meant to be timeless and are ambivalent to whatever stage of the economic cycle we happen to be experiencing. Discipline and patience are the keys to investment success, and these attributes cannot be manifested when we align investment decisions with current events or the latest direction of the stock market.

My hope is that by reading this book and following the precepts found therein, you will be able to free yourself from the burden of following the daily fluctuations associated with your money. Then you will be able to create a plan for yourself, a plan that has the resiliency of the bristlecone pine—a plan that will allow you to fill your retirement experience with those things that are most meaningful to you.

CHAPTER 1

The Best of Times

Woody Allen once said, "More than any other time in history, mankind faces a crossroads. One path leads to utter despair and hopelessness. The other, to total extinction. Let us pray that we have the wisdom to choose correctly." You may get a chuckle out of this quote, but if your life experience was only limited to today's headlines, you could conclude that this quote is entirely accurate.

When I graduated from high school, the news was likewise grim. The population explosion was unstoppable, famine was inevitable, and pesticides were going to give all of us cancer. Deserts were growing and rain forests were shrinking and we were running out of oil. If these maladies didn't do us in, acid rain, the hole in the ozone layer, or the bird flu certainly would. That is, of course, if the nuclear winter didn't kill all of us first.

You may think I'm exaggerating, but a best-selling book written by economist Robert Heilbroner in the seventies concluded that "the outlook for man, I believe, is painful, difficult, perhaps desperate, and the hope that can be held out for his future prospects seems to be very slim indeed."[1]

Now, forty years after the book was published, we can see that every one of these threats has either been a false alarm or has been greatly exaggerated. The forecasted "dreadful future" we have lived through has not been nearly as bad as the "grown-ups" promised it would be. In fact, life on planet earth just seems to be getting better and better for its billions of inhabitants.

Warren Buffet called the babies born today "the luckiest crop in history." I would like to add that the baby boomer generation is the "luckiest crop" of retirees to have ever lived.[2]

By all measurements, the baby boomer retiree is healthier, wealthier, happier, cleaner, kinder, safer, freer, more educated, more equal, more charitable, and more technologically advanced than any previous generation of retirees. Our opportunities are endless. We have more leisure time, we travel more, and we live longer and more comfortably than those before us. During our working careers, the unimaginable happened. Innovation, driven by the mating of ideas facilitated by the internet, has brought about unbelievable progress.

The average person on the planet today earns roughly three times what an individual earned fifty years ago, and that is after inflation has been taken into account. However wealthy you were fifty years ago, you did not own a computer, smartphone, or even a microwave oven. There was no email, social media, or Google. Catching a flight, to even a neighboring state, was cost-prohibitive for most people. Phone calls outside of the immediate vicinity were costly; therefore, most communication happened via the postal service.

Only three television channels were available for viewing pleasure in 1965, but maybe it wasn't that big of a deal because most people didn't

1. Heilbroner, Robert L..*An Inquiry into the Human Prospect.* (New York, W.W. Norton 1974), 22.

2. It is interesting to note that retirement is a relatively new concept. Our parents and grandparents may have had limited retirement experiences, but prior to their generations, our ancestors would work until they couldn't. They would work until they died.

have television sets anyway. Only three channels and no such thing as a remote control . . . awful. If you wanted to see a movie, going to a theater was your only option, because Netflix, DVDs, and even VHS tapes were still in the dream stages. Music selection was limited to choosing a station on the radio or buying a vinyl record to play at home on your record player. The imagineers of Disney's Tomorrowland as well as the animators of *The Jetsons* obviously underestimated the future and were not able to even dream about the comforts that we now enjoy.

Thanks to better techniques, hybrid seeds, and better fertilizers, farmers have provided the earth's population—which has doubled during the last fifty years—with more food than we can eat. The food we do eat is produced by fewer individuals and on a third less acreage. Death from famine has plummeted, and those that do perish by famine tragically do so because of politically caused reasons, not because of a lack of worldwide food availability. The price of food worldwide has fallen steadily over the last 200 years. In 1950, we spent 30% of our household budgets on food. Today we spend a third of that. In most nations, the most prevalent nutrition problem is obesity, not hunger.

Energy is incredibly abundant. The development of horizontal drilling and hydraulic fracturing (fracking) has revolutionized the world in which we live. Just a decade ago, the United States was dependent upon foreign oil to run its economy. Many of the oil-producing countries we were forced to purchase oil from had governments hostile to the United States. We now buy our oil from the good people of Texas and North Dakota, instead of the governments of Iran, Libya, and Venezuela. Just within the last few years, the United States has become the largest producer of energy in the world.[3] The United States is now energy independent and we are retrofitting the ports that we previously used to import oil to export liquefied natural gas to the world.

The world economy has grown at a furious pace, faster than the British economy during the Industrial Revolution, or, for that matter, faster than any nation at any time in recorded history. The U.S. economy

3. *International Energy Outlook 2016-World Energy Demand and Economic Outlook,* Energy Information Administration (Report Number: DOE/EIA-0484 2016) 11 May 2016.

has quadrupled in terms of real GDP in the last fifty years. Worldwide economic inequality is rapidly declining. Why? Because people in poor countries are getting rich faster than people in wealthy countries. Africa is experiencing astonishing growth, like Asia did a decade ago. Mozambique is 60% richer per capita than it was in 2008. Ethiopia's economy is growing at 10% a year.[4]

Amazingly, while this explosive economic growth has been taking place, the pollutants in our world have plunged. In the United States, lead pollution has dropped by 90 percent, carbon monoxide and sulfur dioxide by 50 percent, and ozone and nitrogen dioxide have decreased dramatically.[5] Smog is, for the most part, banished from our cities. Rivers that once were the dumping grounds for industrial waste are once again teeming with life. For the first time since the Revolutionary War, Atlantic salmon are spawning in the Connecticut River and the ultra-sensitive spiny seahorse is back in the Thames. Humpback whales, giant pandas, grizzly bears, and manatees have been dropped off the endangered species list.

Because of advanced warning systems and more durable infrastructures and inventions such as heating and air conditioning, the loss of life from natural disasters and severe weather is at an all-time low. Globally, the probability of death because of drought, flood, or storm is 98% lower today than it was in 1920.[6]

The average person lives about a third longer than they did 50 years ago, and buries two-thirds fewer of their children. A child born today is more likely to live to retirement age than his or her forebears were to live to their fifth birthday. The last decade had the smallest number of deaths

---

4. World Bank- World Development Indicators, World Bank and International Comparison Program <http://data.worldbank.org/indicator/NY.GDP.PCAP.PP.KD> (27 February 2016).

5. *United States Environmental Protection Agency, 'Air quality trends'*, Department for Environment, Food and Rural Affairs <http://www3.epa.gov/airtrends/aqtrends.html> (22 March 2016).

6. Indur M. Goklany, "Wealth and Safety: The Amazing Decline in Deaths from Extreme Weather in an Era of Global Warming 1900-2010," Policy Study 393 (Reason Foundation published report, September 2011).

due to warfare since records began tracking in 1940.[7] Violent crimes are on the decline. There is less murder, rape, theft, and domestic violence, and you are half as likely to die in a traffic accident.

We can all point to countries and situations that are exceptions to the rule, but overall, there is less oppression and prejudice, as well as greater freedom and opportunity worldwide. Not too long ago it would have been inconceivable to consider booking a ski vacation in Russia, visiting the ancient temples of Cambodia, or soaking up the sun on a Cuban beach. This is our new reality.

Technological advancement's greatest deterrent is mankind's inability to imagine. In other words, technology is evolving as fast as we can think of applications for it. We carry more technology in our pockets and purses than the Apollo space program had to send men to the moon. My house vacuums itself while I sleep. My car emails me when it needs air in its tires, and my phone gives me turn-by-turn directions to destinations, even in third-world countries. One ton of freight can be transported 500 miles by railroad on a single gallon of diesel fuel.[8] In 1965 it took eighteen man-hours to create a ton of steel. Today, a ton of steel can be produced using only two-man hours.[9]

Furthermore, technology is evolving faster than we can get regulatory authorization to use it. Google has already developed and has successfully tested cars that drive themselves. Experts estimate that human error causes 90% of all automobile accidents in the United States.[10] Hundreds of thousands of lives will be saved annually when we convert to using these less error-prone cars of the future. Think of the

7. Colin Schultz, "Globally, Deaths from War and Murder Are in Decline: The World is Getting Safer, Even If it Doesn't Necessarily Feel Like It," *Smithsonian Magazine*, 21 March 2014, <*http://www.smithsonianmag.com/smart-news/globally-deaths-war-and-murder-are-decline-180950237/*>.

8. *The Environmental Benefits of Moving Freight by Rail*, Association of American Railroads, (March 2017).

9. *The New Steel Industry*, American Iron and Steel Institute, (Washington D.C: The New Steel, 2006).

10. *National Motor Vehicle Crash Causation Survey: Report to Congress*, U.S Department of Transportation: National Highway Traffic Safety Administration, (Springfield, Virginia: National Technical Information Service July 2008).

life-changing blessing this development will be to the disabled and aged once this technology becomes operational.

Amazon has asked the Federal Aviation Administration for permission to allow their packages to be delivered to their customers by drone. Once the FAA approval is in place, Amazon predicts they will be able to deliver packages to our homes within thirty minutes after receiving an online order.[11] Going shopping will be an option, not a necessity. Now *that* is a life-changing enhancement.

Perhaps the greatest evidence of societal progress is manifested in the health-care industry. Life is just getting better. Cancer deaths have plummeted 25% since 1991.[12] This massive decline in death by cancer can be attributed to earlier detection, as well as enhanced treatments, both made possible through improved technology.

In 2003, scientists announced they had completed a draft of sequencing the human genome. Essentially, they were able to map all the genes that make up a string of our DNA. This genome sequencing has helped identify single genes that cause disease and genetic disorders. Knowing this information has resulted in the creation of better drugs and treatments. New drugs are being developed at an astounding rate. The diseases responsible for killing our ancestors in droves, such as polio, measles, yellow fever, diphtheria, cholera, and typhus, are either eradicated or rare.

Individuals afflicted with genetic disorders now have genuine reasons for hope as treatments continue to evolve. For example, the median survival age for cystic fibrosis was only five years in 1955. Today the median predicted age of survival is 41.[13] It is a very realistic assumption that those born today with this disorder will live long and prosperous lives.

---

11. Amazon Prime Air <*https://www.amazon.com/Amazon-Prime-Air/b?node=8037720011*> (21 March 2017).

12. Susan Scutti, "US Cancer deaths down 25% since 1991, Report says," CNN, 6 January 2017 <*http://www.cnn.com/2017/01/06/health/cancer-death-stats-2017/*>.

13. Ricki Lewis, PhD, *Median Survival in Cystic Fibrosis Soars—Medscape—Aug 20, 2014.*

Not only are we living longer, but we are also living better. Think of the millions of people who have benefited from joint-replacement surgery, cataract surgery, LASIK procedures, the development of pacemakers, and unbelievably advanced hearing aids. Robots and minimally invasive arthroscopic techniques are commonplace in today's surgical procedures. The use of these advanced technologies allows surgeries to be done with greater precision, smaller incisions, decreased blood loss, less pain, and quicker healing. I witnessed the difference in recovery time between gallbladder removal surgery in 1973 and one performed recently. In 1973, the surgery was dangerous, required a large incision, and many weeks, if not months, of recovery time. Now the removal of the gallbladder requires several small incisions, and is usually performed as an outpatient surgical procedure. That's right—the procedure doesn't even require an overnight stay at the hospital. Patients resume normal activity in just a couple of days.

Indeed, we live in amazing times! The most exciting fact is that we are just beginning. The innovations that led to the enhanced lives we now enjoy are but the tip of the iceberg. For the most part, the huge advancements that are outlined in this chapter really happened not over the past fifty years, but in the past ten years. Certainly, future developments in science and technology will only continue to enhance the best retirement lifestyle the world has ever known.

Step One

Recognize the Retirement Challenge

CHAPTER 2

Unprecedented Challenges

"It's paradoxical, that the idea of living a long life appeals to everyone, but the idea of getting old doesn't appeal to anyone."

—*Andy Rooney*

After reading the first chapter you might be thinking I am like the man who falls out of a skyscraper, and as he passes the second floor, shouts, "So far, so good!" Yes, I am an optimist, but also a realist. We truly live in remarkable times, but the retirees of today have challenges to grapple with that no previous generation has had to consider. Ironically, the wonderful advancements and technologies described in the first chapter are the root of the problems this generation of retirees will be facing. Not only are we living better, but we are also living longer. Therein lies the challenge: We are living *too* long.

LONGEVITY

Living a long and prosperous life is a universal dream. But living too long, and becoming dependent upon others for our activities of daily living or financial sustenance, turns the dream of living a long and prosperous life into a nightmare. In fact, a recent poll discovered that retirees are more afraid of running out of money and becoming dependent on others than they are of death!

As previously mentioned, life expectancies are steadily climbing. For the past 200 years, life expectancies have crept up by three months per year. This trend will only accelerate as billions of dollars' worth of research is poured into the development of anti-aging drugs and genetic therapies. In the unlikely event that medical discoveries don't yield any monumental breakthroughs, the gradual increase in life expectancy that has been experienced for two centuries will still give a child born today the expectation of living to 100.

Because of longer life expectancies, many retirees face the very real risk that they will outlive their money if they don't plan for a lengthy retirement. Planning on living to the average life expectancy is not enough. It's best to plan on living longer than your life expectancy, because life expectancy estimates the *average* time a person will live. To be certain, some people will die before their life expectancy, but some will live beyond, sometimes many years beyond, their projected life expectancy.

As you can see from this chart (opposite), a man age sixty-five has a 43% chance of living until age eighty-five, and a 22% chance of living to age ninety. These odds rise significantly for females; a woman age sixty-five has a 55% chance of living until age eighty-five, and a nearly 33% chance of living to age ninety. The scariest thing the life expectancy chart reveals is that there is a 48% chance that at least one member of a couple will live to age ninety, and a 20% chance that a member of a couple will live to ninety-five![1]

Are you financially prepared for a thirty-year retirement?

1. I suggest visiting the Wharton School of Business Life Expectancy Calculator. *<https://www.myabaris.com/tools/life-expectancy-calculator-how-long-will-i-live/>*

LIFE EXPECTANCY AT AGE 65			
To Age:	Male	Female	At Least One Member of a Couple
80	63%	73%	90%
85	43%	55%	74%
90	22%	33%	48%
95	7%	13%	20%
100	1%	3%	4%

Source: Social Security Administration, Period Life Table 2013[2]

Given the probability that our lives will be long, it is essential that pre-retirees and retirees plan their investment strategies to provide income for a prolonged lifetime rather than for a limited number of years. The bottom line is, the greatest financial threat retirees face today is not losing money in risky investments, but outliving their money. Living too long has morphed from a risk into a stark reality, and retirement planning and investing strategies must accommodate this new reality.

ERODING PURCHASING POWER

Longevity is the catalyst for today's retirees' second challenge: their dollars are shrinking. That's right—every day, the purchasing power of the retiree is eroding as the goods and services the retiree consumes are getting more expensive. Although inflation has always existed, no previous generation has had to deal with it to the extent that today's retiree does. Previous generations had shorter life expectancies. Our parents and grandparents lived ten or fifteen years past retirement, on the average, and inflation never had time to develop into a problem. A retirement lasting thirty or more years is a game changer. Therefore, maintaining our

2. *The 2016 Annual Report of the Board of Trustees of the Federal Old-Age and Survivors Insurance and Federal Disability Insurance Trust Funds,* U.S Social Security Administration (Washington, D.C., June 22, 2016) 96

purchasing power, or, in other words, keeping our investments growing faster than inflation, over a three-decade retirement will be a monumental challenge. If the eroding effects of inflation are not recognized and addressed, the future independence and self-reliance of the retiree is in jeopardy.

Inflation is an insidious, sneaky thief that quietly steals your future day by day, year by year, until the once prosperous lifestyle you worked three or four decades to create is gone. The confiscation of wealth by inflation is so stealthy that it happens in broad daylight, right before your eyes. Most victims of theft by inflation don't even realize they have been ripped off until it is too late. Inflation can be likened to gaining two or three pounds every year. In and of itself, it doesn't seem like a big deal, until you wake up one day and realize that you are 100 pounds overweight and facing life-threatening health challenges. Unlike weight gain, inflation is not a risk, or something that *might* happen; it is a reality, something that *will* happen. In my opinion, inflation has confiscated more wealth, destroyed more retirements, and crushed more dreams than the combined effects of all stock market crashes.

Inflation poses a "stealth" threat to investors as it chips away at real savings and investment returns. The goal of every investor is to increase his or her long-term purchasing power. Inflation puts this goal at risk, because investment returns must match the rate of inflation just to break even. An investment that returns 2% before inflation in an environment of 3% inflation will actually lose 1% of its purchasing power. This erosion of purchasing power might seem incidental, but this type of loss, compounded over the duration of a retirement, is life changing.

The effects of inflation caught me by surprise when our old Suburban finally died (yes, I am married to a soccer mom). As I started shopping for a replacement vehicle, I was shocked to find that the cost of a new Suburban was more than I paid for my first house! As I was explaining my plight to one of my ninety-year old clients, he smiled and said, "I understand inflation; I paid $4,000 for my first house." Now that's inflation!

Dollars invested into money market accounts, certificates of deposits, fixed annuities, and bonds never have, and never will, keep up with inflation. Uninformed, anxious, stock market-leery investors that depend on these types of investments for long-term growth may be insulating themselves from stock market volatility, but they are committing financial suicide, slowly but surely. To make matters worse, the paltry gains associated with these products must be taxed, which makes it that much more unlikely that they will be able to preserve purchasing power.

Certainly, there is a time and place for money to be invested in these inflation-susceptible types of investments, but money that is needed for long-term growth must not be invested here.

Recently, inflation has been quite low, but historically, the average inflation rate has been more than 3% annually. To put that into perspective, at a 3% inflation rate, a dollar's worth of purchasing power today will only purchase forty-one cents worth of goods and services thirty years from now. Here's another way of looking at it: In thirty years, at a 3% inflation rate, you will need to have $2.45 to equal the same purchasing power that $1 has today. That means we will be paying $8.50 for a gallon of milk, $17 for a combo meal at our favorite fast-food restaurant, and $100,000 for a new, average-quality, mid-sized car.

In the current environment of huge government budget deficits and spending, it is likely that inflation will continue to rise at least at the same pace as its historical average. Many economists have predicted that inflation will actually exceed the comparatively low inflation rates of recent history. An additional inflation concern is that of health-care related expenses. Retirees spend more on healthcare than any other group, and inflation for health-care related items is growing at double the national inflation rate. Given the one-two punch of longevity and inflation, it is imperative that retirees are mindful of inflation as they invest and plan for the future.

INVESTMENT MANAGEMENT RISK

The third challenge associated with today's retirement is the personal responsibility the retirees now have to manage their own investments. During the last couple of decades, a subtle transfer happened. The responsibility to provide retirement income has shifted from the employers to the employees. The popular pension plans of the past, which guaranteed a lifetime of monthly income to retired employees and their spouses, are disappearing. Consider yourself fortunate if you are a beneficiary of such a pension plan.

Pensions have been replaced by 401(k)s and a variety of similar plans that all have one thing in common: They place the burden of funding and managing investments, to provide a future stream of retirement income, squarely on the employee. The employee bears all the risk in this high-stakes experiment.

The responsibility the employee has of accumulating, properly investing, and then efficiently distributing retirement funds can be daunting. Most are completely unprepared for the task. Few have any training, education, or experience managing investments. No investment plans are followed because there are no plans. Investment discipline is unheard of, as investment decisions are driven by emotions and the daily headlines, which in combination never produce a positive outcome.

Many employee-investors recognize that they don't have the knowledge, temperament, or desire to assume this responsibility that has been thrust upon them. But, no matter what your particular skill set might be when it comes to investment management, the stark reality is that the responsibility to grow a retirement nest egg, and subsequently distribute this money over a thirty-year retirement, belongs to you. You became an investment manager—like it or not. You, and you alone, hold the keys to your financial future.

As you can imagine, with little training or experience, the investing public has proven to be awful investors. An annual study done by DALBAR, Inc. compares the twenty-year average annual rate of return for the overall stock market,[3] with the return realized by those who invest into mutual funds[4] that invest in the stock market. For the twenty

3. as measured by the S&P 500

4. A mutual fund is an investment vehicle made up of a pool of funds. The pool of funds is invested by a manger or team of managers, with the objective of meeting the stated goals of the mutual fund. (If you are a participant in a 401k, you own a mutual fund.)

years through 2016, the stock market averaged 11.96% annualized, while those who invested into the stock mutual funds realized a paltry 7.26%.

Although these two numbers bounced around a lot from year to year, the relationship between them remained constant. Over twenty years, the average stock fund investor managed to capture only 60% of the return of the stock market. Ouch! The largest contributing factor that explains this blatant underperformance was the investor's own behavior. Behavior characterized by irrational exuberance and equally irrational pessimism. It appears that the typical investor followed the herd mentality, buying when stocks were high and selling in a panic when stocks were low. Seldom was the investor guided by a comprehensive investment plan. Therefore, little or no discipline was demonstrated. What is most concerning, is that for the most part, the investor failed at the easy part of investment management: the accumulation phase.

When people enter retirement, they also enter the distribution phase of investment management. In other words, they start withdrawing their investments. The distribution phase is much more difficult to manage than the accumulation phase. In the distribution phase, it is still crucial to know how to properly allocate and invest a portfolio,[5] but additional complexity is added to the mix. Income hungry-retirees need to know how to create a distribution plan that will provide a stream of income that will last until the end of their lives.

There are questions that today's retirees need to answer, questions that were never thought of during the working years, or, for that matter, that no previous generation of retirees ever had to think about:

- Exactly how am I going to turn the lump sum I have accumulated over my working career into a stream of income that will last for as long as my spouse and I live?
- How much do I dare withdraw from my investments?

5. A collection of diverse investments that you put together in an attempt to achieve your financial goals.

- How do I ensure that I don't blow through my retirement savings too fast?
- Am I short-changing my retirement by not paying myself enough out of my retirement funds?
- From which of my investments do I withdraw money to provide income?
- How do I invest my money so I can maintain my purchasing power, but not lose money in the stock market?
- How do I maintain investment discipline during retirement and not make major mistakes during periods of market volatility?
- How do I protect myself from my older self when my financial judgement is clouded by age?
- Am I going to outlive my money or is my money going to outlive me?

Complex investment choices as well as the need to balance inflation risks with stock market risk have made it more difficult for the average investor to be successful in the distribution phase of investment management. Nothing short of a comprehensive Retirement Income Plan, a plan that incorporates all sources of retirement income, will furnish the cash flow necessary to provide for the balance of the retiree's life. The Retirement Income Plan is the core of a financially sound retirement. Although all retirees need a plan, thus far, few have figured out how to create and adopt such a plan.

STEP TWO

DETERMINE PERSONAL RETIREMENT PREPAREDNESS

CHAPTER 3

Are You Prepared to Retire?

"Far and away the best prize that life offers is a chance to work hard at work worth doing."

—Theodore Roosevelt

After you understand the challenges that today's retirees face, the next step is to ascertain if you are ready for this immense lifestyle change. As a registered investment advisor, my professional life is consumed with the creation, implementation, and the oversight of retirement income plans for my clients. During three decades of advising retired clients, I have concluded that financial preparedness for retirement, although essential, is just one part of a very big retirement puzzle. The decision to retire impacts every aspect of your life, so a discussion regarding retirement preparedness is warranted. The emotional as well as financial aspects of retirement preparedness are too important to omit from this book.

EMOTIONAL PREPAREDNESS

I have seen firsthand that, in almost every instance, the emotional impact of retiring is overlooked. We tend to focus on financial preparedness for retirement while allowing the idea of its emotional impact to somehow get lost. Retirement, which completely changes one's financial direction from working and putting money away to not working and withdrawing money, is the single biggest, scariest financial decision that a person will be forced to make. This leap into the great unknown involves the largest sum of money a person has ever had, money that represents four decades of hard work and dedication. It's understandable that, for some, retiring represents one-part money and twenty-parts sheer terror.

ARE YOU PREPARED TO LEAVE THE WORKFORCE?

For many of us, our employment defines who we are. We fulfill important roles as we achieve goals bigger than ourselves. Our employment provides structure to our lives. It gives us a place to be, things to do, and people to see. It gives us a sense of belonging and purpose in the society in which we belong. If retirees can't find activities that provide the same type of emotionally supporting benefits that employment provides, then retirement will soon become a boring and depressing endeavor.

Lee had prepared well for his retirement. He was diligent in saving money during his working years through contributions to a 401(k) and a Roth IRA. Additionally, he had the good fortune of being able to sell the family farm for a substantial sum to developers as the growth of the community expanded to his farm. Lee and his wife, Grace, certainly had sufficient money to provide for a wonderful retirement. Unfortunately, Grace passed away not long after Lee retired.

One day, while passing through Lee's community, I stopped by the local Walmart to pick up a couple of items. To my surprise, Lee, a Walmart employee, met me at the door and welcomed me to the store. Of course, I had to ask some questions. "What in the world are you doing working as a greeter at Walmart? Do we need to adjust how much money you're getting from your investments each month?' Lee laughed and explained to me that his working at Walmart had nothing to do with money; he was bored and lonesome and he missed the social interaction he once enjoyed while employed. He thought he might like greeting his friends and neighbors at the store.

Lee is not alone in his need for social interaction and the desire to get out of the house to do something during retirement. In fact, a study[1] done by Merrill Lynch in 2013 about working during retirement revealed some interesting facts. First, almost 50% of those who retire go back to work. The study found that once people retire, they go through a period of relaxing, refreshing, and retooling that lasts for about two and a half years. Then, they return to the workforce. You might think they go back to work for financial reasons, but the study reveals that rather than making more money, retirees restarted employment for reasons such as staying mentally and physically active, enjoying social interaction, having new challenges, and gaining a sense of identity and self-worth. The study further revealed that less than 50% of those being surveyed returned to the same profession as their primary career, and only 5% chose to work full time. To summarize, half of us, after a break of a couple of years, will go back to work part time for emotionally supportive reasons in jobs that, in many instances, are different from our chosen careers.

Employers have noticed this change in attitude about traditional retirement, and are figuring out ways to both accommodate their retiring employees and profit from the vast experience and knowledge they have to offer. Unique "phased retirement" solutions are being created by many employers. They allow the employee to ease into a decreased work schedule with less responsibility. For both the employee and the employer, this more flexible approach to retirement is turning out to be much better than the traditional "cold turkey" retirement of the past. Phased retirement gives employees the additional time and freedom they feel they need, and the employer retains the expertise of the experienced employee to mentor younger workers.

1. Merrill Lynch. "Work in Retirement: Myths and Motivations." (Bank of America Corporations 2014).

WORKING DURING RETIREMENT

Even though many of us want to keep working past retirement age, or plan on going back to work after we retire, we can't depend on revenue from working to carry us through our retirement years. In other words, even if we plan on working during retirement, that does not exempt us from diligently saving for our retirement. The reality is that the plan to work after retirement is not dependable. Personal health issues, needing to care for a spouse, company downsizing, and outdated skills all contribute to retirees not continuing to work at retirement time or not returning to the workforce after they retire.

THE IMPACT OF RETIREMENT ON THE MARRIAGE RELATIONSHIP

During Richard's working life, he owned three auto dealerships. When he sold his dealerships, he had all the money he needed to fund a wonderful retirement with his wife, Beverly. Shortly after his retirement, however, his wife came home from shopping to find that Richard had completely reorganized her kitchen. Richard had even lined up the spices alphabetically. That was the final straw. Beverly insisted that Richard find something to do. Richard, realizing that his marriage was in trouble and that he genuinely missed the social interactions he had before retirement, started looking for ways to fill his time.

He did find something to do. I met Richard as he was working at his new job, driving a shuttle bus at the local ski resort. He explained that he drives three days a week and skis the days he doesn't drive. In the summer months, he is the golf marshal at the local golf course. He gets to ski and golf for free and, in Richard's words, "They even pay me!" Both Richard and Beverly are enjoying their new retirement arrangement.

No matter how good your marriage might be, spending day after day with even the one you love can be stressful. One of the culprits of marital rift at retirement is that of misaligned expectations. In a study[2] done by Fidelity Investments in collaboration with the Stanford Center of Longevity, it was found that most men look forward to spending more time with their wives in retirement, while the majority of retired women look forward to spending more time with their grandchildren.

In my experience, I have noticed that men often forget that while they were employed, their wives were busy with their own careers, or were busy in or away from home, and developed their own routines, patterns, and social outlets. They certainly don't want or need their husbands restructuring their lives once they retire. Many times, the wife of a newly retired husband has confidentially asked me, "What am I going to do with this guy?"

A healthy dialogue should take place before retirement to outline expectations. Who will do the chores, how much time will you spend together versus being involved in individual pursuits, and what are you going to do with your lives? I believe that we focus too much on answering, "What we are retiring from?" when, the question we should really be answering is, "What are we retiring to?"

ARE YOU FINANCIALLY PREPARED FOR RETIREMENT?

Financially speaking, retirement is an income problem. Are you going to outlive your income or is your income going to outlive you? The challenge of retirement is creating a stream of income that will last as long as you and your spouse are on this earth. The goal is to create an inflation-adjusted stream of income that will satisfy your needs for upwards of three decades. Retirement will be miserable if you lack the necessary income to take care of yourselves until you die.

2. Fidelity Investments *Decision to Retire Research* represents insight from a series of in-depth interviews conducted in Boston, Chicago and San Francisco (April 2015), and an online survey of more than 12,000 defined-contribution plan participants record kept by Fidelity, ranging in age from 55 – 80 across all industries' and income levels, who felt they had some control over their decision to retire. The research was completed in August 2015 by Greenwald & Associates, Inc., an independent third-party research firm. Fidelity also worked in collaboration with the Stanford Center on Longevity on the study.

3 STEPS TO FINANCIAL PREPAREDNESS

1. Create a budget, and figure out how much income you will need.

You would think that people would wait to retire until they've saved enough money or have sufficient sources of income to live comfortably. However, research has found that nearly half of all survey respondents just picked a date when they wanted to retire, and that was that. Their projected future retirement income was not a factor in their decision to retire. That's scary.

To answer the question of how much we need to accumulate for retirement, shouldn't we first determine how much we plan on spending during retirement? The bottom line is that you will need to take some time and create a retirement budget. I understand that this might be a little difficult to do, because you have never been retired before and you don't know how much income you will need. But a well-thought-out guesstimate will be necessary.

As you guesstimate, keep in mind that as a retiree, you will no longer be paying FICA taxes or contributing to a 401(k). Additionally, you will not be paying the cost of commuting, and you may not have to budget as much money toward maintaining a professional wardrobe and dining out as you did while employed. On the other hand, hopefully you will be spending more money on travel, leisure, and recreational activities. There are all sorts of helpful websites and apps available to you as you create a budget. Be generous with yourselves and your projections. Retirement lasts a long time, so don't cut yourself short.

2. Maximize all sources of retirement income.

There are two primary sources of income during retirement: "mailbox money" and income from your investments. Mailbox money is the income you receive on a systematic basis into your checking account such as pensions, Social Security, rental income, and any other source of dependable reoccurring monthly payments. When I started my career, monthly payments from these sources arrived via the U.S. Postal Service.

Thankfully, these payments now arrive electronically, directly deposited safely into our checking accounts. It is hard to break old habits, so please indulge me as I continue to refer to this income stream as "mailbox money."

At retiring time, most retirees don't put as much thought as they should into maximizing their income streams from their mailbox money. For example, more than half of new Social Security recipients elect to start receiving Social Security benefits at age 62, the earliest possible age. However, they can significantly increase their monthly Social Security benefit by simply delaying filing for it for a couple of years.

Additionally, the decision of whether to take a lump sum pension versus electing a monthly pension payment is often not very well thought out. This decision, one that will make a huge impact on the retiree's financial future, is all too often made on the spur of the moment in the benefits office of the soon-to-be former employer.

After you have guesstimated a retirement budget and figured out how to maximize income from your mailbox money, you can see where you stand financially. If income from your mailbox money covers all of your expenses, count yourself very fortunate. With the advent of the 401(k) and the disappearance of the traditional pension plan, fewer and fewer retirees will have sufficient mailbox money to cover all the expenses associated with retirement. Any shortfall will have to be made up from personal investments.

3. Create an income stream from your investments.

The most common question I hear from pre-retirees is, "How much money do I need to accumulate in my IRA and 401(k) before I can retire?" Essentially, they are asking, "How much is enough?" Of course, the answer to that question is determined by calculating how much income your investments need to provide to make up shortfalls in mailbox money income. In later chapters of this book, I will address managing investments during retirement, and how to create a stream of income from investments. For now, I simply want to answer, "How much is enough?"

The rule of thumb used by the financial planning community to determine how much income can be safely withdrawn from retirement accounts is 4% annually. I know that some financial professionals think this is too aggressive. Some will suggest that the retiree can take out more than 4% each year. I feel comfortable using the 4% guideline, as long as the underlying investments are properly managed and well diversified.

So, let's say that you need $80,000 of annual income for retirement, and that your mailbox money will provide $50,000 of that income. Therefore, you need $30,000 of additional annual income from investments. To figure out the lump sum you will need to provide that $30,000 of annual income, you simply multiply $30,000 by 25 and that will tell you the amount of money you will need to accumulate. Therefore, a lump sum of $750,000 will give $30,000 worth of income according to the 4% rule ($30,000 x 25 = $750,000). If you have a lump sum and are wondering how much income that amount will provide, simply multiply that lump sum by .04 and it will reveal how much income you could expect from that sum of money. So, for example, $600,000 will generate $24,000 based on the 4% rule ($600,000 x .04 = $24,000).

Retirement is a very individualized event. Each retiree has their own expectation of what their retirement lifestyle will be. Some retirees hope to travel and be on the move, while others are completely content to spend more time at home, reading a good book, or working in the garden. With so many opportunities, so many choices, retirees must chart their own unique futures. There is, however, one thing that is universal to all retirees: The level of satisfaction with retirement is directly correlated with the level of preparation for this life-changing event.

Step Three

Maximize Income Sources

CHAPTER 4

Maximize Your Social Security

"You can be young without money, but you can't be old without it."

—Tennessee Williams

Past generations took little thought regarding how they would maximize their Social Security benefits. After all, it really didn't matter how and when benefits were claimed if the retiree lived only a short time after retiring. Today, with the real possibility of living three decades without a job or paycheck, retirees need to do all they can to squeeze the most out of Social Security.

Over its almost eighty years of existence, Social Security has evolved. It now consists of hundreds of codes, comprising tens of thousands of pages of rules and regulations. Because of this complexity, most eligible recipients don't understand the benefits they are entitled to receive. Therefore, millions of dollars of Social Security benefits are left on the table each year. For example, a high percentage of Americans apply for Social Security retirement benefits as soon as they are eligible, guaranteeing themselves the smallest benefit possible. Poor decisions are often made when it comes to Social Security, simply because retirees don't know the rules. Instead of basing decisions on facts, they make decisions based on hearsay.

While Social Security is complicated, it is essential to make informed choices regarding both when and how to apply. This will ensure you will get the most from the system. After all, you and your employers have contributed to this future source of monthly income since the day you started working. Now that it's time for you to collect, you owe it to yourself to investigate all the options so you can maximize your particular benefit. Understanding how the system works, and creating an individualized plan to maximize this valuable benefit, could mean the difference in hundreds of thousands of dollars of retirement income.

Social Security retirement income is an especially valuable resource because it provides five important benefits. These benefits make Social Security the anchor of a retirement income plan.

1. *A predetermined amount of income.*

By the time you come to the end of a working career, your Social Security income amount is pretty well known. The benefit amount is based on both your earnings history and when you decide to apply for benefits. The accuracy of the benefit estimation makes it easy to build the rest of your retirement income plan around a reliable number.

2. *Reliable income.*

Once you start getting Social Security benefits, the amount of income you'll receive is set. Some people worry that proposals to reform the system may cause benefits to be cut in the future. That is highly unlikely. To date, there haven't been any proposals that I am aware of that even hint at cutting benefits for those who are already receiving them.

3. *Income that lasts for a lifetime.*

Social Security is one of the few sources of income that can be relied upon for a lifetime. It's an especially valuable benefit, considering the long-life expectancies of today's retirees.

4. *An inflation-adjusted income.*

Social Security benefits are increased each year based on the previous year's inflation rate, which is measured by the consumer price index. These cost-of-living adjustments help retirees keep up with the ever-increasing cost of goods and services.

5. *Survivor benefits.*

Although Social Security checks stop at the death of the recipient, monthly benefits can continue to be paid to surviving spouses and minor dependents.

THE SUSTAINABILITY OF SOCIAL SECURITY

There is a lot of misinformation that surrounds the sustainability of Social Security. This misinformation comes from two different sources: People who want to scare you into buying precious metals that will "be there for you when the dollar is worthless," and politicians who want to win your vote by demonizing their incumbent opponent that is "single-handedly responsible for the United States being more 20 trillion dollars in debt." Because I neither sell precious metals nor am running for a political office, I have no ulterior motive other than to just tell you the boring truth: Social Security is not going away anytime soon.

Each year, the Congressional Budget Office (CBO) reports to Congress the fiscal status of Social Security.[1] The latest report states that if no changes are made to the system, the Social Security Trust Fund, along with income collected from our taxes, will allow Social Security to pay all its obligations until the year 2034. If no adjustments are made to the Social Security system between now and 2034, there will only be enough money in the system to pay 77% of the promised obligations after 2034.

Minor adjustments to the system now could extend the viability of Social Security for years into the future. Raising the age requirements of

1. *The 2017 Annual Report of the Board of Trustees of the Federal Old-Age And Survivors Insurance and Federal Disability Insurance Trust Funds,* The Board of Trustees of the Federal Old-Age and Survivors Insurance and Federal Disability Insurance Trust Funds (Washington D.C.: U.S. Government Publishing Office 2017) 6.

future claimants, changing how the cost of living adjustment is calculated, or raising the maximum earnings subject to the Social Security tax are all viable measures that should be considered to strengthen Social Security. To date, these common-sense solutions have not been implemented because anytime a politician has suggested a change to Social Security it has proven to be a political boondoggle. Like any financial problem, the sooner we address these future projected shortfalls, the easier they will be to manage. Making decisions about claiming Social Security benefits based on the false assumption that these benefits are disappearing is both dangerous and irresponsible.

ANSWERS TO SOCIAL SECURITY QUESTIONS

Below, I have listed the ten most commonly asked questions regarding Social Security retirement benefits. The answers to these questions can be found on my website, *petersonwealth.com,* on the "Resources" tab.

I have chosen to answer these questions on my website rather than in this book so I can adjust the answers as the Social Security Administration alters its rules and regulations. Social Security is a living, changing entity that has adapted, and will continue to adapt, to societal changes. Accommodating the challenges associated with increased life expectancies will require modifications to the current system. There will inevitably be changes to the current system and I will do my best to keep the answers to these questions current on my website.[2]

- How much can I expect to receive?
- What if I apply for benefits between the ages of 62 and full retirement age?
- What if I apply for benefits after my full retirement age?
- How do cost-of-living adjustments (COLAs) affect Social Security benefits?
- When should I apply?

2. *www.petersonwealth.com*

- Is my spouse eligible for a Social Security check based on my own work history?
- How do divorced spouse benefits work?
- What happens to Social Security benefits when the working spouse dies?
- Can I receive Social Security benefits while I am employed?
- How are my Social Security benefits taxed?

A NOTE ABOUT MEDICARE

Medicare is the national health insurance program for people over the age of 65 and for those under age 65 who are receiving Social Security disability benefits. Participation is mandatory if you want to have health insurance in this country. While you can and should purchase private supplemental insurance that covers the gaps in coverage that Medicare does not cover, you must enroll in Medicare first before the supplemental insurance can take effect.

When you turn 65, Medicare becomes your primary insurance provider. That means all secondary insurance policies that you may have will not pay any claims until Medicare has paid its share. It used to be that most retirees would apply for Social Security at or before age 65. They would usually sign up for Medicare at the same time. Now, a growing number of retirees are electing to delay the application for Social Security benefits after age 65 to increase their future Social Security benefit amounts.

Regardless of when Social Security benefits are first collected, you need to apply for Medicare at age 65. If it is not applied for at age 65 (it is recommended to start the application process three months before turning 65), a 10% penalty will be added to the Part B premium for each twelve-month period that it is not applied for. For example, if applying at age 67, there is a 20% penalty that is added to the Medicare Part B premium for the rest of a retiree's life.

There is always an exception to the rule. The exception to the rule when comes to signing up for Medicare is, that if you or your spouse are still working and have access to group health coverage, you are exempt from signing up for Medicare until after you are retired. Once retired, you have eight months to sign up for Medicare before the 10% penalty will be assessed.

Here are the five most important things to remember about Medicare:

1. *Medicare is not automatic.*

Everyone has to sign up for Medicare. (If Social Security retirement benefits are started prior to age 65, Medicare will automatically kick in at age 65).

2. *Medicare will not start until age 65.*

Regardless of whether Social Security benefits are collected before age 65, Medicare will not start until age 65. If no employer coverage is available, private insurance is needed to cover the gap.

3. *Medicare is not free.*

The cost for Medicare is deducted monthly from Social Security payments. Medicare does not cover everything.

4. *Medicare supplemental insurance is available.*

Medicare supplemental insurance is available to cover what Medicare does not cover and is sold through private insurance companies. These policies must be applied for within a specified time. Medicare.gov has a list of the policies available, including their prices and features, and retirees can shop for these plans according to the medications they are taking.

5. *Medicare does not cover long-term care.*

Custodial costs, or the costs associated with stays in nursing homes and assisted-living facilities, are not covered by Medicare. Long-term care insurance must be purchased separately from a private insurance company to cover these types of costs.

Social Security is responsible for 42% of today's retirees' income. While it does not provide enough income to retire on, it does provide a solid foundation upon which a sound retirement income plan can be built. The decision to start Social Security does not happen in a vacuum. This decision affects all other aspects of the retirement income puzzle. Social Security, along with other mailbox money and retirement funds, should be integrated into a plan to create a stream of income that will last for decades. A little time and effort can pay significant dividends when deciding when, and how, to receive Social Security benefits. I strongly encourage you to visit my website as well as the Social Security website to learn more and to figure out the best strategy to maximize your Social Security benefits.

SOCIAL SECURITY RESOURCES

For answers to Social Security questions, go to *www.petersonwealth.com* and click on the "Resources" tab.

Click on the "Retirement Planner" on the *www.socialsecurity.gov* website for assistance with any of the following:

- Estimate your benefits
- Request a Social Security statement
- Compute the effects of early or delayed retirements
- Apply for benefits online
- Locate a Social Security office
- Get answers to your questions

CHAPTER 5

Maximize Your Pensions

"Live long enough and you'll come into pensions, a lovely thing. Presents every month from people you didn't know cared."

—Ruth Gordon

Past generations of retirees didn't have a lot of choice when it came to how they would structure their retirement income. They had Social Security and their guaranteed monthly pension checks from the employer they had dedicated thirty years of their lives to. Almost 80% of their income came from these two reliable sources of mailbox money. These pension plans that guaranteed a monthly benefit are called "defined-benefit plans." Defined-benefit plans provided the retiree with a degree of income certainty that most of today's retirees are missing.

The problem is, defined-benefit pension plans are disappearing. In 1983, there were 175,000 of these types of plans in the United States;

today, there are less than 45,000.[1] For those over age 75, pensions are the norm. For workers under age 35, pensions are virtually non-existent. Consider yourself fortunate if you are a participant in one of these plans.

Defined-benefit pension plans are becoming extinct for three reasons:

1. *Defined-benefit pension plans became too burdensome for most employers to undertake.*

The decline of the defined-benefit retirement plan began in the 1970s when the government tried to rectify abuses it saw in corporate America. They did this by passing the Employee Retirement Income Security Act (ERISA). While ERISA has deflected most of the corporate abuses over the years, it also introduced many complicated laws that are hard to comply with. To avoid dealing with the politics and complexities of ERISA, many companies decided to do away with pension plans. They were never a mandatory offering for companies, and it was easier to do away with the plans than to conform to ERISA's complex regulations.

2. *There is a tremendous liability to companies that provide defined-benefit pension plans.*

Companies that offer these plans must, by law, provide current retirees their pre-determined retirement benefit every month, even if the investment fund the pensions are paid from has done poorly. Pension payments, especially during turbulent economic times, have the potential to put a company out of business. Simply stated, most companies do not think the risk, the cost, and the difficulty of maintaining a defined-benefit pension plan are worth the effort it would take to establish and maintain the benefits for the employee.

"Defined-contribution plans," which consist of 401(k)s, TSAs, 403Bs, and a variety of other pretax contribution plans, have taken the place of the old defined-benefit plans. From an employer's standpoint, these plans are cheaper and less difficult to manage. By adopting the

1. U.S. Department of Labor. "Private Pension Plan Bulletin Historical Tables and Graphs 1975–2014" (Employee Benefits Security Administration, published report, September 2016).

defined-contribution plan, employers have effectively transferred the entire responsibility of funding, managing, and distributing retirement funds from themselves to their employees.

3. We have become a much more mobile society.

Gone are the days when an employee worked for one company for an entire career. Defined-benefit plans rewarded the long-term employee with a monthly retirement check, but these rewards came with a cost—not of money, but of time. The price to be eligible for these plans was decades of loyalty to a single company.

The 401(k)s of today are much better equipped to deal with the shorter duration that most workers commit to a single employer. Even if employees work for an employer for a short amount of time, they can roll 100% of their contributions to a new 401(k), or to an IRA, upon terminating employment with the employer.

PENSION INCOME

If you participate in a defined-benefit pension plan, you will have to make some irrevocable decisions when you decide to retire. These decisions all have to do with survivor pension benefits for your spouse. You'll need to answer this question: Should I take the highest monthly pension check available and leave my spouse with no monthly pension income when I die, or should I take a reduced monthly check upon retiring in order to leave my spouse with some kind of a monthly income? This decision is important and, once you make a choice, is irrevocable.

If you or your spouse has a relatively short life expectancy, then take that into consideration when choosing which pension option is right for your family. If other assets are available (life insurance or investments) to provide your surviving spouse income after your death, then taking a reduced pension at retirement to provide income for your spouse may not make sense.

Be thoughtful about decisions regarding survivor benefits, and choose what is best for your situation. Be ingenious and don't limit your choices to what is presented to you in the human resource department the day you retire.

LUMP-SUM PENSION PAYOUTS

Many pension plans allow the retiring worker to elect a lump-sum distribution of their pension proceeds in lieu of systematic monthly payments. The lump-sum payment can be rolled into the retiree's IRA and, if transferred correctly, will not be taxed until money from the IRA is distributed.

So, what is best, guaranteed monthly payments for life, or a lump sum of money? There are obviously several factors to consider when making this important decision. Some of the factors revolve around your propensity to manage money. If you tend to be an emotionally driven investor and have proven to make poor investment decisions in the past, or if you can see yourself blowing through a lot of money in a short amount of time, even for worthy causes, then a monthly pension payment might fit your situation best.

But generally, the lump-sum pension option is the best way to proceed. Every family situation is unique, and every company structures their benefits differently. In almost every situation, however, the math favors the retiree rolling their pension over to an IRA. Do the math in your own situation, and consider the following reasons for rolling your lump-sum pension into an IRA:

1. A lump-sum pension rollover puts retirees in charge of their own money and financial destiny.

The retiree, not the pension plan, decides how money is invested and distributed. Monthly pension payments come from a pool of money managed by the pension plan. Many pension plans don't have sufficient money under management to pay projected obligations; or, in other words, they are underfunded.

There are many underfunded pension plans in the United States. In fact, the latest studies[2] indicate that pension plans across the United

2. Milliman, "2017 Corporate Pension Funding Study," (published report, Milliman 2017).

States are underfunded by 325 billion dollars. Therefore, the Pension Benefit Guarantee Corporation (PBGC) was established—to provide protection to the millions of American workers who are now (or will soon be) getting a monthly pension payment. The PBGC guarantees pensions much the same way the FDIC guarantees bank deposits. Even though the PBGC could provide some protection if pension plans run out of money, the PBGC coverage is limited, and will not be able to cover all the pension payments promised to retirees. For this reason, I would suggest that you take some time to research the financial health of your own pension plan, and make that information part of the decision-making process.

2. Monthly payments from pensions do not keep pace with inflation.

Pension payments typically do not have a cost-of-living adjustment like Social Security does. These payments will not keep up with inflation. According to the government's CPI Inflation Calculator,[3] a $4,000 pension check thirty years ago has the purchasing power of only $1,871 today. Imagine taking a 53% cut in pay! That is the effect of inflation. Due to inflation, monthly pension checks received late into retirement aren't nearly as attractive as they may have initially appeared.

3. Once monthly pension benefits are elected; pension payments cannot be adjusted to provide for emergency situations. However, once a lump-sum pension's funds are rolled over to an IRA, that money can be accessed to provide lump sums in the event of a crisis.

You may ask, "When would I need a large lump sum?" There are several situations that could require a large amount of money, or more money than a monthly pension payment would provide. Having a lump sum of money can open alternatives when it comes to custodial care later in life. Lump sums would be necessary if a life-saving organ transplant were required for you or a loved one. Additionally, when a spouse dies

3. U.S. Bureau of Labor Statistics., <*https://www.bls.gov*> (1 May 2017).

and family income is disrupted, it is to your advantage to have options—options besides being locked into a monthly pension payment.

4. It can be tax-wise to roll pension funds into an IRA.

Systematic monthly pension benefits are taxable, and cannot be stopped once elected. If the retiree does not need monthly income from the pension, unnecessary taxation will result. It makes more sense to roll the pension into an IRA to continue to grow tax-deferred, rather than receiving unneeded monthly (and taxable) distributions. Lump-sum pension payments are still subject to required minimum distribution rules when you are at age 70½, but complying with these rules still gives you more flexibility in managing your investments and taxes than receiving a monthly pension payment.

In 2016, the IRS approved a provision in the tax code regarding Qualified Charitable Distributions, or QCDs. This provision allows individuals, once they are age 70½, to gift IRA monies directly to qualified charities. These gifts count toward satisfying annual required minimum distribution (RMD) specifications. This allows individuals who are charitably inclined to gift their required minimum distributions directly to charity, without having to add the RMDs to their taxable income. This provision opens tax-planning opportunities where taxes on Social Security benefits could be reduced, and the need for filing an itemized deduction could be eliminated. Because of the new QCD provision, other tax-saving strategies beyond the scope of this book could be implemented for the charitably inclined (please talk to your tax advisor for details). The point I want to convey is that gifting opportunities and other tax-saving strategies could be thwarted by not electing a lump-sum rollover.

5. If a monthly pension distribution is selected, and the pension recipient(s) dies soon after retiring, no benefits are payable to heirs.

In other words, heirs receive nothing if a monthly payment is chosen and the pension recipient(s) die prematurely. It would be a shame to elect a $3,000 monthly pension payment and forgo a $300,000 lump-sum rollover, only to die in the early years of retirement. The family of the retiree, or their favorite charity, would have missed out on $300,000. Only pension plans benefit from the retired employees' premature deaths.

Lump-sum rollovers can be a valuable asset that, if properly managed, can create both a lifetime of income and a potential lump-sum benefit to the retiree's heirs. It is important to note that pension plan funds must be rolled directly to an IRA, or a 20% withholding tax will be deducted from the distribution. Additionally, the entire distribution is taxable. This is a fatal tax mistake. If you do not feel comfortable with this process, I would recommend you run, not walk, to a qualified financial professional to help you navigate this transaction.

Pension plans, whether in the form of monthly payments or lump-sum distributions, are a valuable bonus to a retirement income plan. This money, like all other streams of income, should be integrated into a well-thought-out retirement income plan.

CHAPTER 6

Income from Investments

"Money, which represents the prose of life, and which is hardly spoken of in parlors without an apology, is, in its effects and laws, as beautiful as roses."
—Ralph Waldo Emerson

At retirement, once you have made thoughtful decisions about how to get the most out of your mailbox money, the balance of your retirement income will have to come from your investments. The distribution of your investments will need to be coordinated with your mailbox money for tax purposes, as well as to help you stretch these dollars out to last as long as you do.

You may have been a very successful accumulator in IRAs or 401(k)s over your working career, or you might not have accumulated much at all. Whatever your situation, I promise you that investing and properly distributing your retirement nest egg over the balance of your lifetime will be much more challenging and less forgiving than accumulating retirement funds.

I liken the accumulation and distribution of retirement funds to what a skier experiences at a ski resort. Riding the chairlift up the mountain is the easy part of skiing. It takes no skill, and even the most inexperienced skier can ride the lift without running into too many difficulties. The skier simply must stay on the lift and they will get to the top of the mountain. Just one warning: Abandoning the lift could prove to be fatal.

Having a 401(k) is like riding the lift. A certain percentage of a worker's check is systematically deducted by an employer, oftentimes matched, and then deposited directly into an investment portfolio. It's easy, even automatic. But, as abandoning the ski lift could prove to be fatal, not participating in a 401(k), or failing to invest into an IRA, will have catastrophic consequences.

With almost absolute certainty, new skiers crash as they get off the lift for the first time. I certainly did, and every first-time skier I have been with has crashed exiting the lift. The initial getting-off-the-lift crash is surely followed up with several dozen additional mishaps throughout the first miserable day of skiing. Getting down the mountain can be extremely frustrating, and even dangerous to the novice skier. Help from an experienced instructor is invaluable.

Likewise, new retirees often make mistakes as they begin retirement, crashing, so to speak, as they make poor choices regarding their Social Security and pensions. These decisions in and of themselves can damage a retirement, but a continual stream of bad investment decisions can crash even the best-funded retirements. Choosing the proper mix of investments and properly liquidating an income stream from the right type of investment is the key.[1]

---

1. The views expressed are those of the author and not a recommendation to buy or sell securities, or of any particular asset allocation strategy. These investment guidelines are not intended to represent investment advice that is appropriate for all investors. Each investor's portfolio must be constructed based on the individual's financial resources, investment goals, risk tolerance, investing time horizon, tax situation, and other relevant factors. Please discuss with your financial advisor before implementing an investment plan.

ACCUMULATION VERSUS DISTRIBUTION

So why is distributing retirement funds so much more difficult than accumulating funds?

One only must go back to the decade 2000–2010 to understand how volatility in the stock market[2] impacts the accumulator, versus someone who is retired and is distributing retirement funds. As a reminder, the years 2000–2003 were awful years for equities.[3] The year 2000 was the infamous bursting of the dot-com bubble, when the overpriced technology stocks of the 1990s retreated on a large scale back to realistic valuations. Billions of dollars of equity were erased in a short period of time. This difficult correction was soon followed by the tragic events of September 11, 2001, when the financial center of our country was the target of the worst terrorist attack ever perpetrated on American soil.

The stock market declined by 49% between 2000 and 2003 before recovering.[4] From 2004–2007, the stock market finally gained some momentum, until the worst market downturn since the Great Depression hit us in 2008–2009 (declining by 57%). The net result for the U.S. stock market was that it ended the decade in 2010 at about the same level as it started the decade in the year 2000. Ten years without growth. The good news is that since the market's low point in 2009 to the time of the writing of this book, the stock market has increased by more than 300%.

You might ask, how did this volatility and ten years of no growth affect the accumulator? Well, it was a wonderful blessing! Those of us who were systematically contributing to our 401(k)s and IRAs from

2. Throughout the book when I refer to stocks or the stock market, I am talking about stocks in the broadest sense: the universe of stocks as opposed to any one company's stock, or even a few stocks. I am generally referring to the S&P 500, which accounts for roughly three-quarters of all the value of all the publicly traded stocks in the United States.

3. I use the word "equities" interchangeably with stocks because it is an all-inclusive word that refers to all investments that can hold stock. Besides direct ownership of shares of stock, mutual funds, exchange-traded funds (ETFs), and variable annuity sub accounts that hold stocks are considered equities. Most investors are exposed to the stock market through these products.

4. U.S. stocks fluctuate in price so that the value of an investment can go down depending on market conditions. Stock prices may fluctuate due to stock market volatility and market cycles, as well as circumstances specific to a company.

2000–2010 were able to purchase greater quantities of equities as the price of stocks plummeted during the decade. Certainly, our account balances suffered temporarily, but as the share prices dropped, the number of shares we were able to purchase rose as we systematically purchased beaten-down shares of stock month by month. Once we had accumulated a bunch of cheap shares over the decade, the stock market shot up to record highs. Those downtrodden stocks we purchased so cheaply during the "lost decade" have now caused our account balances to explode with value.

This contrasts greatly with what happened to the unfortunate retiree who was distributing during the first decade of the century. Many of those investors were forced to sell their equities at the worst possible time. They had no choice; they had to sell at a loss to provide the income necessary just to pay the bills. Many well-funded retirement accounts were devastated during this turbulent time.

Systematic purchasers of equities do well investing in declining markets, while systematic liquidators of equities are crushed during down-market cycles. During 2000–2010, buyers were blessed, and sellers suffered. This decade perfectly illustrates the difficulty of managing and distributing retirement funds versus simply accumulating retirement funds. The good news is that there are plans that can be implemented to help protect future retirees from having to liquidate equities at a loss to create income, should you be unfortunate enough to begin your retirement at the beginning of a bear market.[5] I will introduce such a plan to you in the last chapters of this book.

THE NEED FOR GROWTH

As I remind you of the turbulent first decade of this century, you may be thinking, "I will just avoid equities altogether so I won't be forced to liquidate these volatile investments in a down market." Sorry, that won't work. Remember, keeping ahead of inflation is essential to having enough income to last throughout retirement, and equities are one of

5. A bear market is defined by at least a 20% retreat in the overall stock market index from its previous high point.

the few investments that have proven to beat inflation over the long run. If maintaining your retirement lifestyle and preserving purchasing power is the objective, equities will be a necessary component of your portfolio. There is no way to get around them.

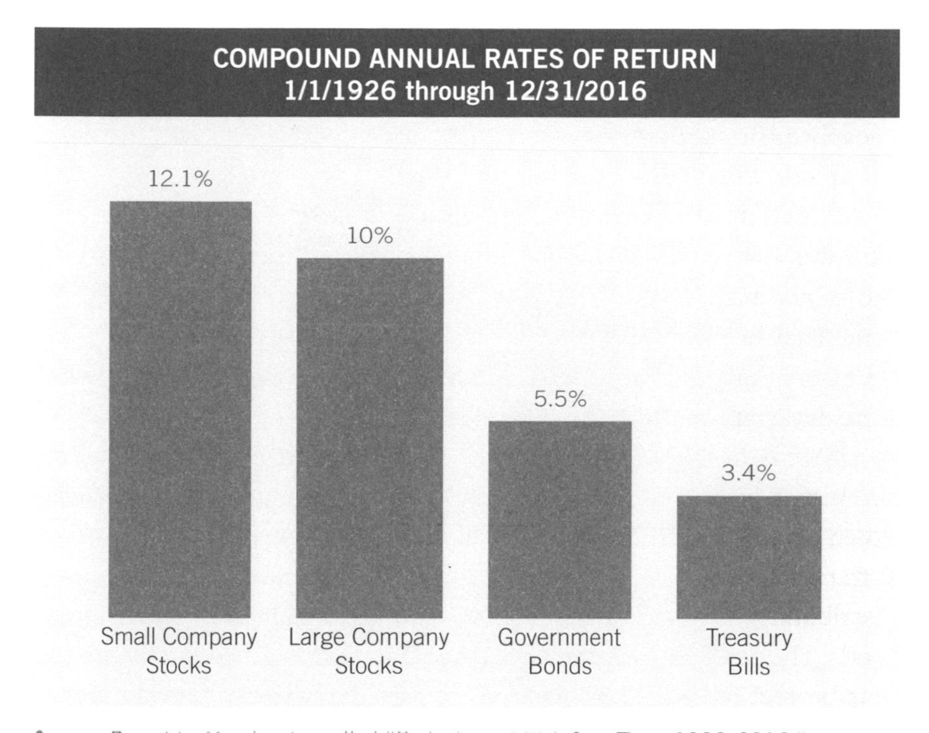

Source: Report by Morningstar called "Reduction of Risk Over Time, 1926–2016."

As I see things, there are only two types of investments: fixed income investments and rising income investments. Fixed income investments are characterized as slow growing and non-volatile investments such as bank deposits and bonds. Certainly, there is an appropriate time to own fixed income investments. They should be the investment of choice when you have a limited time for your money to grow (less than five years) and you can't afford to wait out a stock market correction. Fixed income investments protect us from short-term volatility but are damaging to own over the longer term, as they offer little protection against the erosion of purchasing power.

In the long run, the only rational approach to protect against the erosion of purchasing power is to invest in rising-income type investments, in other words, owning equities. As a shareholder, or the partial owner of some of the greatest companies in America, you have the rights to the profits those companies make. These companies pay their shareholders their proportional share of the profits in the form of dividends. Historically, the dividend rate of the greatest companies in the world, or the S&P 500,[6] has increased about one and a half times faster than consumer prices have gone up. In other words, they have managed to stay ahead of inflation. Besides the growth of dividends, historically, stocks have experienced a tremendous amount of growth in their value.

STOCKS, BONDS, AND COMPOUND INTEREST

Government bonds[7] are the classic fixed-income investment. They are very stable and are backed by the federal government. For the last thirty years, these bonds (as measured by the ten-year treasuries) have had an average annual return of about 5%. If $100,000 were to have been invested into these bonds in 1987, the value of that investment would be $460,000 today.[8]

Meanwhile, stocks, the classic rising-income investment, have averaged almost 10% for the same time. $100,000 placed into an investment that mirrors the S&P 500 for the past thirty years would be worth $1,650,000 today.[9] Even though the stock portfolio gained double the annual interest rate than the bonds did, it created more than three and

6. The Standard and Poor's 500 Index (S&P 500) is an index of the 500 largest U.S. publicly traded companies and is an indicator of the performance of the overall U.S. stock market.

7. Although bonds are significantly less volatile than stocks, bonds are not risk-free investments. The two main risks related to bond investing are interest rate risk and credit risk. Typically, when interest rates rise, there is a corresponding decline in the market value of bonds. Credit risk refers to the possibility that the issuer of the bond will not be able to make principal and interest payments.

8. Calculated using starting date January 1987 and ending date January 2017 using the Treasury Return Calculator <*https://dqdj.com/treasury-return-calculator*>

9. Calculated using starting date January 1987 and ending date January 2017 using the S&P 500 Return Calculator <*https://dqdj.com/sp-500-return-calculator*>

a half times the value over thirty years! That is the magic of compound interest. We will be talking more about compound interest in Chapter 11. For now, what you need to know is that inflation-beating growth is necessary to maintain your purchasing power over retirement, and that kind of growth is achieved by investing into equities.

For most investors, the stock market is not clearly understood. I am continually surprised by the lack of understanding the public has on how the stock market works, what its historic returns have been, and the risks involved with investing in equities, or, better said, the risks involved by *not* investing in equities. It seems like this general lack of understanding is not isolated to the least educated among us. Rather, stock market illiteracy cuts across all socioeconomic classes. Some of the best-educated, smartest people I have ever been associated with are bewildered when it comes to understanding and investing in equities.

A reminder might be in order. When you purchase a share of stock, you become a partial owner of the company whose stock you purchased. As an owner of the company, you are entitled to all of the profits and growth associated with that company, according to the proportional amount of the company that you own. The stock market is not some nebulous or abstract concept that is impossible to understand; rather, it is the marketplace where buyers and sellers of shares of corporations come together. The value of a particular company's share of stock is determined by the sellers and buyers agreeing on a price where they can exchange their shares of stock. It's really that simple.

Land, cars, homes, and essentially anything that can be bought and sold on the open market will have a price that fluctuates. The price fluctuates because the point where a seller is willing to sell, and the point where a buyer is willing to buy, is constantly changing. Buying and selling partial ownership or shares in corporations is no different than buying and selling anything else, but somehow the simplicity of the concept is lost when it comes to buying shares of stocks.

During the financial crisis of 2008–09, I was reviewing investments with a cattle ranching client. Obviously, things weren't looking very good with his portfolio because of the worldwide sell-off of stocks that was occurring at that time. My client suggested that maybe he should sell his equities and put the diminished proceeds in the bank.

I asked the client what the price of cattle was at that time, and he informed me that the cattle prices were likewise awful. I asked him if he was going to sell his herd of cattle and put that money in the bank also. His response was classic: "I can tell you don't know much about the cattle business. You don't sell cattle when the price is low! You just have to be patient and wait for cattle prices to rebound. Now let's get back to talking about these stocks. Do you think we should sell?"

My ranching friend is not alone when it comes to treating equity transactions differently than buying and selling other assets. I can't even tell you how many times I have had people tell me, after a market downturn, that they were not going to buy equities until things stabilized a bit and prices rebounded. That is like saying, "I'm not interested in buying that cabin for a 30% discount; real-estate prices are just too uncertain. When cabin prices stabilize, and the price goes back up 30%, I will write you a check." We wouldn't conduct any of our other business in this manner. Why do we treat our equity purchases differently?

I believe that part of the problem is that equities inform you their selling price daily. I promise you that if the price of your home was listed in the newspaper every day, you would have been tempted into selling your home three or four times during the last twenty years. Thankfully, the price isn't listed every day, so you didn't sell, and look where the price of your home stands today.

Having a partial ownership of the greatest companies in America has always been the long-term solution to staying ahead of inflation. As I write this book, I am thinking of the corporations whose goods and services I used just today, corporations that are making money on me, today. I wanted to share a list of all the corporations whose goods and services I use in a single day, but as I was compiling my list, I realized that it would contain possibly as many as 100 companies. I patronize multiple corporations in various sectors of the economy, including utility, energy, finance, transportation, agriculture, manufacturing, and health care, to name a few. And you likewise do business with these companies. Why are we worried about owning them? They are the best-run, most profitable companies the world has ever known.

Certainly, the daily selling prices of these corporations fluctuate, but being an owner of a diversified portfolio of these corporations over a long period of time has been, and I believe, will continue to be, the recipe for success.

Equities are an essential component of a successful retirement income plan, so we might as well address "stock fiction" in the next several chapters to diffuse some of the misconceptions and misinformation that surrounds this topic. This information will be especially important, since you will need a part of your retirement funds invested in equities, if protecting purchasing power is your objective.

Step Four

Dismiss Investment Fiction: Welcome to the Grand Illusions

As an investment advisor, as well as one who has extensively researched investment-related topics over the past thirty years, I have come to a disappointing conclusion. The ideas embraced and promoted by many in the investment industry and the media are not shared by the facts that are revealed in the academic world. This section of the book is dedicated to debunking the investment fallacies of our day by exposing where academic research and conventional wisdom collide. We really can't proceed with a constructive discussion about the management of investments during retirement without first dispatching false investment narratives.

So, why is there a chasm between academia and the messages shared by the conventional investment pundits of the day? The simple answer is that for some, profits trump giving quality investment information. It is important to remember that financial institutions were created to make profits for themselves and their shareholders, not their customers. These entities as well as the financial media are in the business of selling products and making profits. Giving useful, common-sense, factual investment advice is not their objective; selling a product and making money is.

Unfortunately, the tried-and-true facts resulting from academic research are valuable, but usually boring. Fictional concepts, no matter how useless and sometimes damaging they may be, certainly have more sizzle, and sizzle sells products. The financial media, whether it's newspapers, magazines, radio, or television, must "sell" you the news instead of giving you the truth. All news outlets would go out of business if they headlined the simple truths of investing, such as "Patience and Discipline, the Keys to Success," or "Slow and Steady Wins the Race." To survive, they must continually come up with new and exciting headlines to grab your attention with headlines like, "Six Hot Funds to Buy Now!" or "Wall Street's Secrets Revealed!" These headlines are catchy, and I'm sure they generate a lot of money for their companies, but this type of information doesn't help the investor.

I don't begrudge corporations trying to make a profit in the most capitalistic industry on earth. Certainly, there are reputable companies that have valuable products and services we can benefit from. Unfortunately, some companies and individuals fill the airways and printed media with half-truths and even outright lies as they attempt to get us to purchase their products and services. Products and services that are often damaging to the unsuspecting consumer's financial well-being. Just as pornography is harmful to all that get caught in its snare, this financial pornography likewise has no redeeming value, gives the investor a false sense of reality, and will devastate the financial future of any that allow themselves to be seduced by it.

As I searched for a name to call these investment falsehoods, my classic-rock radio station gave me exactly what I was searching for. The old Styx hit "Grand Illusion" started to play and I thought to myself, "Of course." The investment deceptions of our day are indeed grand illusions.

The next four chapters will reveal the four grand illusions of the investment world, as well as identify the individuals and companies that profit from promoting this financial fiction.

CHAPTER 7

GRAND ILLUSION #1
MARKET TIMING

"It's not what you don't know that hurts you. It's what you know that just ain't so."

—Satchel Paige

The "grand illusion" of market timing presupposes that those who are smart enough, or follow the markets closely enough, can figure out both when to get into the stock market and when to get out. The goal is to miss the pain and experience the gain.

Of course, we would all love to own equities and enjoy the profits while avoiding the downturns, but unfortunately, it can't be done. The difficulty in market timing is that you not only have to know when to get out, but also when to get back in. Therefore, you must guess correctly not only once, but twice for market timing to actually work. Like probably every other person who manages money, or, for that matter, has money invested, I have searched for the "holy grail" of market timing.

Certainly, some brilliant person or program somewhere must have figured out how to do this!

Sadly, my research found that of all the financial products I thoroughly vetted, no person or system has proven to be able to figure out how to *reliably* time the markets. I beg of every audience, in every venue in which I speak, to please share with me the name of any person or entity that can reliably and consistently time the stock market. If I could find that magic person or formula, I could retire and trade my podium in for a fishing pole. Unfortunately, my public plea has not provided any credible answers or solutions.

What I have found is that there are a lot of people and products willing to take money from the public who attempt to time the market, but none have a proven track record to substantiate their claims. I have heard it said that, "Buying at the bottom and selling at the top is typically done by liars."[1] My research and experience, validates that statement. Of course, there is the occasional "investment guru" that may guess the temporary movement of the market (remember, even a broken clock is correct twice a day). When that happens, they have their face on the cover of the financial magazines and show up on the financial radio and television shows, but they are soon forgotten. Why? Because successful market timers must guess correctly twice: when to get out, *and* when to get back in. That can't reliably be done.

I often run into individual investors that report to me they saw the financial crisis of 2008–09 coming, and that they were able to avoid the big downturn in the stock market. My immediate response to them is, "That's great—so where is your money now?" Inevitably, they inform me it is still sitting safely in the bank. My response is, "So you are telling me that you missed the 50% downturn, as well as the 300% *upturn* since 2008–09, and you are feeling good about this?" Again, you must guess correctly twice.

1. Skousen, Mark. *The Maxims of Wall Street,* Second Edition. Forecasts & Strategies, One Massachusetts Ave. NW, Washington, DC 20001.2013,193.

On my website[2] I have provided references to academic papers that substantiate what I am telling you, but for now let's look at the mutual fund industry for some logical insight.

CAN YOU REALLY OUTPERFORM THE STOCK MARKET AVERAGE?

The S&P 500 is a representative basket of the 500 largest corporations in the United States: Apple, ExxonMobil, Proctor, Gamble, etc. It is an index[3] that gives us a way to measure how the overall stock market is faring. There is no management of the portfolio of stocks that make up the S&P 500, and you can't buy into the S&P 500 itself. You can, however, purchase exchange-traded funds (ETFs)[4] and mutual funds that mimic the holdings of the S&P 500. When you buy an investment product that mimics the S&P 500, you are becoming a partial owner of all 500 corporations that compose the S&P 500. You are buying a piece of the entire basket of stocks.

The alternative to passively investing into an index fund is to attempt to make money by investing into actively managed portfolios. Actively managed investment portfolios are those that attempt to outperform an index, such as the S&P 500, through market timing and superior investment selection. It is interesting to note that, on an annual basis, only about 15% of actively managed mutual funds[5] that invest into large U.S. stocks can outperform the S&P 500. Let me put it another way. Of all the large-stock mutual funds, only 15% can beat the unmanaged conglomeration of stocks that is the S&P 500. Only 15% can beat the average. You may be thinking that you only need to do the research and find the 15% of mutual funds that beat the S&P 500. That is a great idea, but it's just not

2. *http://www.petersonwealth.com*

3. A market index measures the value of a group of stocks or investments that belong to a pre-defined group i.e. The S&P 500, measures the value of the 500 largest publicly traded corporations in the United States. There are multiple indexes to be found both domestic and foreign, that track the performance of stocks, bonds commodities etc.

4. An exchange-traded fund (ETF) is a diversified investment product that is similar to a mutual fund that tracks an index.

5. June 2016 mid-year report. S&P Dow Jones Indices, SPIVA U.S. scorecard.

that simple. It's never the same funds that beat the S&P 500 year after year. Every year there will be a different group of mutual funds that outperform. You would have to determine in advance which 15% of mutual funds would be next year's winners. Therein lies the challenge. Good luck.

This reminds me of a time when my wife and I were raising our young family. Josh, our two-year-old, had a favorite sippy cup he had to drink out of every day. If he didn't get his special cup, he would have a fit, throw himself on the floor, and cry for an hour. So, it was important that Josh got his special cup each day. The challenge was that his favorite cup changed daily. Some days it was blue, some days yellow, and some days red. Even as his parents, we had no way of knowing in advance which special cup of the day it was going to be. Josh was too young to communicate to us which cup he wanted, so we just had to guess and hopefully, for the sake of peace in our home, guess right. Once in a great while, we would guess the cup of the day correctly. But most of the time, our best efforts were dismal failures according to Josh. Josh is now in medical school and he has yet to start a family, but I look forward to the day when he has a stubborn little child of his own. As a grandfather, I will see that his children have many colored sippy cups to pick and choose from. It just seems like the fair thing to do.

The moral of this story is, whether picking the index-beating mutual fund or tantrum-preventing sippy cups, it's impossible to be successful in selecting the prize of the day when the prize is constantly changing.

In a given year, only 15% of all large stock mutual funds can beat the index, or the stock market average. Over longer time periods, the percentage of actively managed mutual funds that can outperform the index diminishes dramatically. The obvious question that needs to be asked, therefore, is, "Why don't I just buy the average?" Well, why don't you? You can buy mutual funds and ETFs that mimic the index, or the average, for minimal cost.

Trying to beat the index is a loser's game. Timing the market is basically playing poker with the best players in the world, who play around the clock with nearly unlimited resources. When the best and brightest minds of the investment industry can't outperform the index—with all the resources they possess—chances are, you won't be able to beat the index either.

The good news is that you don't need to "beat the market" to be a successful investor. You only need to own it and participate in its earnings. You only need to buy the average, because when it comes to investing, getting the average return of the entire market puts you near the top of the class.

To be clear, there are many stock markets and many corresponding indexes. The S&P 500 represents only the 500 largest U.S. corporations. Besides large corporations, there are mid-sized corporations and small corporations. There are also international large, medium, and small corporations. All of these corporations belong to their own index. Portfolios that aim to mimic these indexes can be purchased through corresponding mutual funds and ETFs. These varying types of equities can and should be used to construct a diversified investment portfolio. (We will discuss diversification in greater detail later in the book.)

THE PROFITEERS OF MARKET TIMING

So, who stands to profit from the "grand illusion" of market timing?

First, the mutual fund industry in general. The fees for actively managed mutual funds are more than ten times higher than buying a fund that mirrors an index. The average cost of actively managed large-cap stock funds is 2.33%[6] when expense ratios and transaction costs are considered. The average cost to buy a fund that tracks the performance of the S&P 500 itself is .20% when transaction costs and expense ratios are considered. Even though index funds outperform actively managed mutual funds and are cheaper to buy, for the obvious financial benefits, mutual fund companies promote their more expensive, worse-performing funds instead.

6. Roger Edelen, Richard Evans, and Gregory Kadlec, "Shedding Light on 'Invisible' Costs: Trading Costs and Mutual Fund Performance," Financial Analysts Journal 69:1 (January 2013).

The second group of profiteers of this particular grand illusion is any other person or entity that promotes the idea that they know what the market's next move will be. Any company or advisor whose value propositions are their knowledge of the future, are co-conspirators of this illusion. Magazines, newsletters, and cable news stations that predict the future of the markets, the price of oil, the next recession, or any other future price or event, likewise share in this "grand illusion."

The following that some of these prognosticators have is amazing. On the air, these self-assured individuals are incredibly convincing. But being convincing doesn't mean they are accurate. Few investors take time to investigate the track record of those that can "see into the future." If you were to Google the accuracy rate of their past predictions, you would know better than to follow their forecasts.

Some of the most entertaining promoters of this illusion are the authors of books that have figured out when the "financial apocalypse" will begin. For $34.99, they will share this dark secret with us, and instruct us on how we can thrive while the entire economy collapses, dollars become worthless, and our neighbors starve to death in the streets.

The next time you are in the bookstore, check out the books on investing. You will find a book authored by Harry Dent in 1999. His book, *The Roaring 2000s,* predicted that the Dow Jones Industrial Average would surge to 35,000 by the end of the next decade. That never happened. Instead, the first ten years of this century ended up being the worst decade for investing since the Great Depression. The Dow Jones Industrial Average closed the decade lower than where it began, an entire decade with no growth.

Instead of taking a breather after this forecasting disaster, in 2009, Mr. Dent doubled down on his forecasting and wrote a new book, *The Great Crash Ahead.* Since this book hit the shelves, the S&P 500 has tripled in value.

It seems like this forecaster just can't get things right. I wouldn't be so disparaging about this author if it weren't for the fact that he continues to be one of *the* most quoted "experts" in the financial industry. Every year for the past several years, he has predicted that the Dow

Jones Industrial Average will drop by 6,000 points. It hasn't happened, but that's not the point. The point is that every time he makes this dire prediction, he sells a lot of books.

The grand illusion of market timing is reminiscent of the California gold rush. In 1849, fortune seekers from across the globe flocked to California in hopes of striking it rich. Fortunes were made, but it wasn't the hard-working prospector that became wealthy. Rather, it was the shop keepers, suppliers and bankers who were the real profiteers. Similarly, fortunes are now being made by market timing. Unfortunately, it's not the investor that will be bringing home the profits. It is the mutual fund industry, brokerage firms and the financial media that are the real winners. With the illusion of market timing, everybody makes money but the investor.

CHAPTER 8

GRAND ILLUSION #2
SUPERIOR INVESTMENT SELECTION

"Don't struggle to find the needle in the haystack. Just buy the haystack."
–Jack Bogle

The fallacy that the stock market can regularly and consistently be outperformed by superior investment selection is the ugly stepsister to Grand Illusion #1 (market timing), and it deserves its own condemnation. The notion that through an extensive search of the stock market or the mutual fund industry, investors can reliably uncover the next investment superstar is categorically false.

People think, "If I could only find and buy the next Apple, Google, or Amazon stock in its infancy, I would be rich." Well, you would be rich, but it's unlikely you will be that lucky. There are thousands of mutual fund managers and pension plan managers, and a wide variety of other highly educated, experienced professionals in the investment industry scouring the investment universe day by day, hour by hour, in search of the next investment superstar. You are competing with the best and the brightest of the investment world. The full-time professionals, with their vast resources, can rarely find a hidden investment gem or concoct a superior portfolio of investments, that can reliably beat their corresponding index (or the average).

I like to think that trying to get rich through individual investment selection, versus owning a diversified portfolio of equities, is like betting on a single football team that will win next year's Super Bowl, versus having a partial ownership in the National Football League (NFL) itself. Owning a share of the entire NFL would entitle you to a proportional share of all of the profits from the entire organization and from every team. Certainly, teams within the organization will experience their ups and downs each year, but overall, the NFL as an entity makes a lot of money (and half of its teams are guaranteed to have losing seasons). A rational investor would not bet on a single team instead of owning a piece of the whole organization. Rational investors recognize that the odds are not in favor of those who try to beat the markets through superior investment selection.

I enthusiastically invite all readers and all who attend my speaking events to introduce me to a person or an investment program that can reliably outperform the market average over the long run, through superior investment selection. Again, my public pleas have gone unanswered. Successful long-term stock and mutual-fund pickers are hard to find. There are no market timers or stock pickers listed among *Fortune* magazine's richest people in the world. Wouldn't you think that if market timers and stock pickers could really do what they claim to be able to do, they would be numbered among the world's wealthiest individuals? So, where are they?

Some would argue that the oft quoted billionaire Warren Buffett would qualify as a successful stock picker. He is a unique and talented investment manager and has made excellent individual investment choices. But Warren Buffett's successes can be attributed to his extreme discipline and patience rather than flipping stocks or timing markets. It is interesting to note the instructions he gives to the trustee of his own estate regarding how his wife's money is to be managed upon his demise: "the trustee is to put 10% of the cash in short-term government bonds and 90% in a very low-cost S&P 500 index fund."[1] We should probably pay attention when the third wealthiest person on the planet shares with us the instructions on how he would like his estate managed.

An additional illustration of Mr. Buffett's belief in the passive investing process is demonstrated in an interesting wager that he made in 2007 with Ted Seides of Protégé Partners. Protégé Partners is a New York–based money-management company that prides itself in its ability to time the markets and outperform the stock market through superior investment selection. The bet was, that for a ten-year period, Protégé Partners would choose a combination of "timing and selecting" types of investments to beat Warren Buffett's choice of a mutual fund that mimicked the S&P 500. At the end of ten years, the winner's favorite charity would receive one million dollars.

At the time of writing this book, the wager had just completed its ninth year. If both had invested a million dollars, Protégé Partners' actively managed funds would have gained $220,000. Warren Buffett's investment into the S&P 500 would have gained $854,000. At this stage of the wager it would be impossible for Ted Seides to win, given the overwhelming lead that Warren Buffett has accrued. I am sure Buffett's charity, Girls Inc. of Omaha, is looking forward to opening the mail next January.

There is a lesson to be learned from this wager. Warren Buffett, one of the smartest investors on earth and one of the wealthiest men in the world, believes in the value of passive investing. He believes very few investors "can beat the market" and he trusts that investing into the average through index mimicking equities will ultimately beat out those who seek above average investment results through superior stock and mutual fund selecting.

1. Warren E. Buffett, Berkshire Hathaway, Inc. 2013 Annual Report, p. 20.

So, who stands to make a buck promoting Grand Illusion #2, that superior investment selection is a viable market-beating strategy? Well, you will find that many of the same characters that profit from the market-timing illusion are also those that profit from the superior-selection illusion: mutual fund companies, brokerage firms, and any entity or individual whose value proposition is their ability to tell you what tomorrow's star investment will be. Especially egregious profiteers in this illusion are the magazines that provide lists of "the best mutual funds for the year" and the television programs instructing the public on what stocks to buy and sell as part of some pathetically inept day-trading strategy.

There is an inordinate amount of time, energy, and money that is wasted on the possibility that the grand illusions of market timing and superior investment selection may contribute to investment performance. The academic world refutes the claims that the grand illusions of market timing and superior investment selection have any significant impact on actual investment results. In practice, the additional costs (increased management costs and higher trading costs) incurred by those who willingly pay for these illusions far outweigh any possible benefit they might offer.

I am continually amused at the naïveté of some investors, who think that if they spend an hour or two every other month checking out stocks, or mutual funds, on the internet, they can create an investment mix that will outperform market averages. When long term, index beating, investment selection can't be accomplished by the most experienced professionals, it is doubtful that the amateur on an occasional cruise through cyberspace will be successful.

Certainly, there is a lot of money being made by the illusion of superior investment selection. Unfortunately, we once again see that everybody but the investor is making that money.

CHAPTER 9

GRAND ILLUSION #3
THE PERSISTENCE OF PERFORMANCE

"If past history is all there was to the [investment] game, the richest people in the world would be librarians."

—*Warren Buffett*

If you have ever bought shares of stock, a bond, or shares in a mutual fund, you were presented with the following disclaimer: **"Past performance does not guarantee future results."** The U.S. Securities and Exchange Commission requires it. As hard as it is for me to admit this, the bureaucrats in Washington actually have this one right. There truly is no correlation of an *individual investment's* past performance and its future performance. Past performance has no predictive power whatsoever.

Of course, that doesn't mean your investment advisor sat you down, rested a hand on your shoulder, and with a kind but concerned look in his eye, uttered these words. No, it was in the fine print somewhere that most of us never bother to read. Or worse, when we came across this disclaimer, we ignored it, because frankly, we didn't want to accept it. We like guarantees. When we buy an investment, we simply want the assurance that it will perform as it has done in the past. Unfortunately, that promise can't *honestly* be given.

The illusion of persistence of performance is hard to diffuse, because so much of our life experience is based on the reliability of past performance. We believe the sun will come up tomorrow morning at the appropriate time, because it always has. We therefore assume that it always will. Your summer vacation at the beach, or next winter's ski getaway, can be planned months in advance because of the persistence of performance of the weather, and the reliability of the change of the seasons. I have a car that has averaged seventeen miles per gallon since I purchased it four years ago. It would be crazy to assume it will average anything but seventeen miles per gallon next month. Persistence of performance surrounds us, and it seems quite natural to want to use past performance as a criterion to select our investments. Unfortunately, there is no evidence that the past performance of a specific investment has any predictive power of that investment's future.

S&P Global,[1] an independent research company that monitors the mutual fund industry, produces a biannual report they call the "S&P Persistence Scorecard." In these annual reports, they always come to the same conclusion: that over a five-year period, less than 1% of the mutual funds in the top quartile at the beginning of a five-year period have been able to maintain their top quartile status at the end of five years.

Many investors waste an inordinate amount of time and energy studying past investment returns, attempting to discover next year's investment champions. It's an exercise of futility, but it's easy to get caught up in, because we really want this illusion to be true. I cut my teeth in the investment business in the late eighties and early nineties, back in the day when double-digit investment returns were the investment norm. It seemed as if the whole world was consumed with finding

1. SPIVA Reportcard *http://us.spindices.com/documents/spiva/spiva-us-mid-year-2016.pdf*

the hottest-performing mutual fund. As a young and inexperienced advisor, I spent countless hours identifying all the top-performing funds so I could direct my clients to them. I now recognize that perfecting my golf swing or cleaning my garage would have yielded equally productive investment results.

So, who profits from promoting Grand Illusion #3, persistence of performance? As I mentioned, this illusion comes to us quite naturally because of our life experience. Nevertheless, any entity that touts their ability to direct you to a superior investment, based on that particular investment's past performance, perpetrates this grand illusion. The Morningstar, Inc. star-rating system for investments is based on past performance, rendering their system meaningless. That's right: buying a five-star fund versus a one-star fund does not increase your chance of success! Countless newsletters and magazines are sold as they flaunt their recommended lists of the hottest stock or best mutual funds to buy. All their recommendations are based on historical performance, and historical performance has no predictive power.

Just as the road in front of us is different from the road behind us, it's important to recognize that drivers as well as investors who navigate solely by what they can see in their rear-view mirror are not well equipped to manage the inevitable twists and turns of the road that lies ahead.

CHAPTER 10

GRAND ILLUSION #4: Equities Are Dangerous and Should Be Avoided

"Fear has a greater grasp on human action than does the impressive weight of historical evidence."

— *Jeremy Siegel*

It happens all too often. I receive a phone call or an email from a nervous investor who has been surfing the internet or watching their favorite news network. They've come across an article, a headline, or an advertisement proclaiming that the stock market is poised to drop by some cataclysmic amount. Further, the advertisement promotes the idea that the stock market is a high-stakes gamble, a roll of the dice, and is certainly rigged against the "Little Guy." I am told that these warnings must be credible. "After all, they are advertised on Fox News," and these warnings "are all over the internet!" It's an amazing phenomenon to watch the power of the media as it turns otherwise rational people into devout believers that the apocalypse is on our very doorstep.

The purveyors of this brand of financial pornography are especially troubling. They prey on the uninformed and the most anxious investors of our society. They dupe the very investors that probably have the greatest need to own inflation-beating investments. Scaring the already apprehensive investor into purchasing high-commission products that will "keep their money safe" from stock market corrections is their modus operandi. Certainly, their articles, advertisements, and headlines are provocative, and are sure to get your attention. They are masters in the art of deception as their message distorts reality and is damaging to those who fall under its influence.

Anybody who understands investing knows that, in the long run, the only way you will be able to maintain the purchasing power of your money is to become a partial owner in a collection of the most profitable companies the world has ever known. In other words, you must own equities if beating inflation is your objective. The price the investor pays for superior, inflation-beating returns is short-term volatility. The stock market has been and always will be volatile. Those who are deceived by the grand illusion that equities are too risky and must be avoided fail to discern the difference between volatility and risk. Few people can make this distinction, but that is precisely the reason why few investors prosper.

VOLATILITY VS. RISK

Volatility is the advent of a temporary decline, while risk refers to the chance of a permanent loss. Properly understood, "volatility" is merely a synonym for unpredictability: it has neither negative nor positive connotations. Let me share with you an example that might help you to distinguish between volatility and risk.

My family's favorite vacation destination is Lake Powell. We own an old houseboat that we share with several other families. I have learned, through experience, that the most important safety precaution I must attend to at Lake Powell is the proper anchoring of our boat. I will sometimes have our boat tethered to four or five anchors at a time. Why? The

Lake Powell area regularly experiences sudden and powerful thunderstorms. These storms come complete with white caps, driving rain, and microburst winds that are capable of sinking both large and small boats. While the storms are volatile and scary, they last but a short time. If you are properly anchored, you will be safe. If a boater is prepared for the volatile storms, there is no damage to life or property.

Risk is when there is possibility of experiencing a permanent loss. Volatility only contributes to a permanent loss when poor decisions are made. Many inexperienced boaters have sunk boats because they were not prepared, they were not properly anchored. They panicked in a temporarily volatile situation and let their emotions rather than sound judgment rule the day.

Financial storms, such as stock market downturns, are likewise frightening, but they, too, last but a short time. The experienced, anchored investor is prepared for the frequent, volatile gyrations equities give us. The unprepared and emotionally driven investor will turn a temporary volatile financial storm into a permanent loss by panicking and selling equities at a loss. Remember, volatility itself does not lead to losses in the equities markets; rather, it's the emotional reaction to volatility that ultimately leads investors to lose money in the stock market. In the world of investing the anchor is having a plan. Having a plan to follow in times of market turmoil reinforces discipline and self-control to the prepared investor.

THE ANATOMY OF A BEAR MARKET

A bear market is a drop of about 20% in value from a specific market's previous high. Bear markets are as common as dirt. As you can see from the chart on the next page, in the seventy-two years since World War II, there have been 13 bear markets. They come around about every six years on average. These declines vary in their severity, frequency, and duration, but on average, the stock market retreats a little over 30% in a bear market. They last on the average about 15 months, then the stock market rebounds and moves on to new highs. Given the very real possibility that your retirement could last two or three decades, you'll be a participant in five or six bear markets during your retirement, so you might as well get used to them.

BEAR MARKETS		
Start Date	Percent Return	Duration in Months
May 1946	-30%	36.5
August 1956	-22%	8
December 1961	-28%	6.5
February 1966	-22%	8
November 1968	-36%	18
January 1973	-48%	20.5
September 1976	-19%	17.5
November 1980	-27%	20.5
August 1987	-34%	4
July 1990	-20%	3
July 1998	-19%	1.5
March 2000	-49%	30.5
October 2007	-56%	17
AVERAGE:	-32%	15

Source: J.P. Morgan, *Guide to the Markets* as of June 30, 2017, pg. 14.

The biggest issue with bear markets is fear. Not fear of what the stock market is doing, but fear of what the investor is doing. Peter Lynch, the fund manager for the highly successful Fidelity Magellan Fund throughout the nineties, said, "The key to investing in stocks is not to get scared out of them." You must not abandon equities when they are down because as sure as bear markets are to come, bull markets[1] will surely follow.

1. A bull market is defined by a period of positive returns in a stock index over a given period.

THE BULL MARKET

I have also included a chart that shows all the bull markets since World War II. As you can see, most investors are missing the point. Instead of worrying about avoiding the next -30% bear market, we should focus our attention to making sure we participate in the next 300% bull market!

BULL MARKETS		
Start Date	Percent Return	Duration in Months
June 1949	265%	87
October 1957	86%	50
June 1962	80%	44
October 1966	48%	26
May 1970	73%	32
October 1974	73%	24
March 1978	62%	33
August 1982	229%	61
December 1987	65%	31
October 1990	302%	95
August 1998	60%	19
October 2002	102%	61
March 2009	258% **	99 **
AVERAGE:	131%	51

** As of June 2017
Source: J.P. Morgan, *Guide to the Markets* as of June 30, 2017, pg. 14.

"The stock market is a highly efficient mechanism for the transfer of wealth from the impatient to the patient" said Warren Buffett. And when it comes to exhibiting investment discipline, Warren Buffett is an excellent exemplar. On Black Monday in October of 1987, Buffett's equities plunged $347 million in a single day (back when $347 million was a lot of money). During the bursting of the dot-com bubble from 2000–2003, Buffett's portfolio again plunged. This time he was down $6.2 billion. That's billion with a "b." And then, during 2008–2009, Buffett's accounts plummeted $25 billion. But the most amazing thing about these seemingly horrific downturns is that, Warren Buffett never lost a penny from those enormous market swings, because he didn't sell.

As mentioned in a previous chapter, it is an exercise in futility to try to guess when to be in or out of the markets. The key is to be disciplined and to stay invested. Since 1945, or the end of World War II, the S&P 500 has averaged an annualized rate of 11%[2] including dividends. Another way of looking at this, if[3] you could have invested $1,000 in the S&P 500 in 1945, that $1,000 would have grown to more than $1,800,000 today. A handsome reward for staying invested.

THE MASTERS OF MISINFORMATION

Instead of teaching the public the virtues of investment discipline and sharing a historical perspective of investing in equities, the promoters of this grand illusion of equity endangerment design advertising campaigns to reinforce the irrational fears of the financially ignorant. The peddlers of this illusion want you to think that volatility and risk are the same. They want you to sell your investments, lock in your losses, and invest in their high-commission products. They fail to explain, and possibly fail to understand, that a diversified portfolio of U.S. stocks has never gone down without fully recovering in a relatively short period of time. Nor do they reveal that in a diversified portfolio of stocks, such as the S&P 500, the only way to lose money is to sell when the stock market is down. Not so coincidentally, this is exactly what they suggest you do to free up the cash to buy their "safe" products. The promoters of these sleazy

2. This is an annually compounded return of the S&P 500 from May 1st, 1945, to June 30th, 2017, with dividends reinvested.

3. The S&P 500 is an index and not an investment. You can't invest into it. However, there are many investment products that mimic the S&P 500 that can be invested into.

enterprises profit only when you panic. They win only when you choose to lose.

So, who are the promoters that benefit from this grand illusion? The answer is simple. Any entity that benefits from frightening people out of equities is a co-conspirator. The companies that profit when you panic are predominantly the sellers of precious metals, annuities, and newsletters with the financial media assisting as a loyal partner in crime. For as they say in the news business, "If it bleeds, it leads." Frightening, sensational, and exaggerated headlines and stories touting the demise of the stock market are the tools they employ to promote their ratings.

PRECIOUS METALS

The thinking is that if, for whatever reason, countries and their currencies cease to exist, then precious metals will be one of the few items that will hold value and preserve purchasing power. My question is, "To purchase what?"

If all the currencies of the world had no value, the world would be in utter chaos. Anarchy and revolution would rule. This has never happened on a large scale in the history of our world, so nobody has a credible idea of what a world without currency would look like. There would be no manufacturing, no food production, and no police or armies to protect us. There would be no commerce—that's right, stores would be shuttered. Why would anybody choose to work if there was not a way to be paid for labor rendered?

So, even if your ounce of gold held its value, what could you buy with it? Where? How? I believe a homemade meal would be worth more than an ounce of gold, if you were fortunate enough to locate the food and a willing cook to put it together for you.

Doomsday predictions and conspiracy theories have never been a friend of the disciplined investor and I simply refuse to fan that flame. If, however, you are one of those who thinks that chaos and revolution are the destiny of our society, you might as well put this book down and get back to building your bunker. But before you go, I would like to share with you one important thought. The richest men in the world, from every generation, did not get that way by betting against the ingenuity and indomitable spirit of the human race to create a better life for itself. Successful investors have always been richly rewarded for their willingness to invest in the future. This generation is no exception. Today's optimists, or those willing to invest in a better tomorrow, are thriving.

For those of you who are not planning on living in a bunker, but are considering owning some gold, "perhaps as an insurance policy or an inflation hedge," let me share with you some facts.

First, although touted as an inflation beater, gold does not keep up with inflation. In 1980, the price of gold was $850 an ounce. The price of gold declined over the next twenty years and bottomed out at less than $300 per ounce at the start of the new millennia. It then shot up during the first decade of the century, peaking at over $1,800 per ounce in 2012, and now has settled back to about $1,200 per ounce.

With all its volatility, gold has gone from $850 an ounce to $1,200 an ounce over thirty-seven years. That works out to be a rate of return of less than 1% per year. Meanwhile, the cost of goods and services, or inflation, grew by 3.1% annually. That doesn't seem like keeping up with inflation to me.

Precious metals are advertised as safe havens from the turmoil of the stock market, yet they are neither safe nor dependable. The price of gold and other precious metals are extremely volatile. In fact, the price of precious metals has historically been more volatile than the stock market. I have a hard time understanding why anyone would want to own any investment that fluctuates wildly in price, never pays a dividend, has a dismal track record and can't keep up with the price of goods and services.

So, when well-known actors advertise that they buy gold because they are "good Americans concerned about the future," please try to see through the deception. They tell you to buy gold because they are actors who get paid to tell you to buy gold.

INDEX ANNUITIES

Index annuities are products created by insurance companies. They advertise that through their product, you can participate in some of the returns of the stock market in the good years but that you will not lose money in the years when the stock market retreats.

The sales pitch of these products is enticing, but the devil is in the details. First, these products have caps or limits on how much they will pay when the stock market goes up. So, when the stock market goes up, earnings within these products are limited to the prevailing cap of the product. If the stock market goes up 10, 15, or even 30% in a given year, these products will pay only the prevailing market cap. In most instances, these caps can be changed by the insurance companies without warning. The consumer has no say. The prevailing market cap at the time this book went to print was around 5%.

Second, these products have severe penalties if you liquidate your investment before the surrender period expires. Surrender periods are imposed because the insurance companies that create these products pay a large upfront commission to the insurance agents who sell these products. If an annuity owner cancels their annuity before the surrender period expires, the insurance company can recoup the commission paid to the agents from the surrender charge assessed to the annuity owner. The surrender periods typically last seven to ten years. Surrender charges can run as high as 10% of the value of the annuity.

Third, index annuities don't participate in the dividends of the stocks in the indexes they follow. This is significant. Almost half of the returns of the S&P 500 can be attributed to the dividends of the underlying companies that make up that index. So, if you choose to invest into the stock market via an index annuity, you automatically cut your profits in half by foregoing future dividend payments.

To better illustrate the absurdity of these products, let's apply the same investment criteria used in an index annuity to a real-estate transaction.

The deal would go something like this: "We will take your money, and invest it into a rental property. Your investment is guaranteed to never lose money, as long as you leave the money with us for at least ten years. If you liquidate prior to ten years, you will be subject to a surrender charge as high as 10%. We get to keep all the rental income stemming from your investment, but we will pay you a *portion* of the annual increase of the value of your property each year, and this amount will be completely up to our discretion. Oh, and by the way, thank you for paying me an upfront commission of 7% of your purchase. It's been a pleasure doing business with you."

Of course, nobody would agree to a real-estate deal like this! Why would we agree to these same terms with our other investments? There are hundreds of index annuities to choose from, and they all have variations on how they credit earnings and apply surrender charges. Even though all index annuities are different, they share a common trait. Index annuities are complicated products and are very difficult to understand. I have yet to meet an owner of an index annuity that seems to really understand how their annuity really works. I believe if the consumer really understood how index annuities work, they would never purchase one.

Before investing any money into an equity index annuity, do your homework and understand how these products are structured. Regulatory organizations empowered by the federal government to ensure that the American investor is protected, have additional information and alerts regarding index annuities.[4]

WHAT ABOUT THE GUARANTEES?

The draw to these products is their guarantees. The only positive guarantee that index annuities offer is that you won't lose money when the stock market goes down. Since every market downturn is temporary, that isn't much of a guarantee when you consider all that you lose by owning these products.

4. *https://www.finra.org/investors/alerts/equity-indexed-annuities_a-complex-choice*
https://investor.gov/additional-resources/news-alerts/alerts-bulletins/investor-bulletin-indexed-annuities

Owning an index annuity will certainly render guarantees—undesirable guarantees:

- It guarantees that you will never get stock market–like returns. Market caps ensure this will never happen.
- It guarantees that you will never be able to beat inflation over the long run by investing into their annuity, again thanks to market caps.
- It guarantees that you just paid one of the highest commissions in the investment universe to the insurance salesman who sold you the annuity.
- It guarantees that you will never be paid a dividend. Dividends historically account for almost half of the gains of the stock market.
- It guarantees that the bulk of your money will be locked up inside one of these products for as long as a decade. Certainly, lump-sum distributions are available to you if you are willing to forfeit as much as 10% of your principal to access your money earlier than what is allowed by the annuity contract.

So, why are these products so prevalent? Unfortunately, they pay some of the highest commissions of any product in the investment industry. Need I say more? Additionally, no securities license is necessary to sell index annuities. An insurance license is all that is needed. Therefore, index annuities are sold by insurance agents, and for many agents, index annuities are the only product in their quiver that could loosely be called an "investment."

Unknowing investors buy these products because they don't understand the difference between volatility and risk. Those who purchase index annuities have been duped by the emissaries of gloom that promote an irrational fear of equities, and fear is a powerful tool. A tool so powerful that the impressive weight of historical evidence manifesting the inflation-fighting power of equities is ignored and traded for a promise that your money will not go down in value when there is a temporary downturn in the stock market.

The grand illusion that equities are dangerous and must be avoided is promoted by those who willingly ruin the future of others to gain a commission. As you have already sensed, I have little regard for those who profit from the most vulnerable individuals of our society, the financially ignorant and the overly anxious.

CONCLUSION

After going over the four grand illusions of investing, you might be thinking I am condemning the entire investment industry. I am not. Certainly, there are those within this industry who are unscrupulous and dishonest. Unfortunately, those types of individuals can be found in every industry, in every community. But the vast majority of financial advisors that I know are good people sincerely trying to help others. Some of these good people may disagree with my assessment of the four grand illusions of the investment world, and may refute my assessment. I respectfully disagree with their heartfelt belief and beg of them to show me a long-term track record to prove me wrong. Thirty years of research and managing money tells me that I won't be contacted any time soon.

Step Five

Understand the Determinants of Growth

Now that the grand illusions of investing have been dismissed, the next step is to answer the question that is begging to be asked: "What are the determinants that drive investment performance?" Fortunately, this question has been bantered about for years and there are credible answers. An overwhelming amount of historical data is available to draw conclusions from, and business schools across the fruited plain have used this data to provide valuable insight on what really drives investment performance.

The most notable research regarding this topic, research that has withstood the test of time, is the landmark study[1] done by Brinson, Hood, and Beebower. Their research concludes that 93% of investment returns are attributed to asset allocation. Simply stated, asset allocation is how money is invested. So, whatever asset class you have your money invested into—whether it be stocks, bonds, real estate, or something else—determines the growth of your portfolio. An asset class can be described as a group of economic resources that share similar characteristics, such as risk and return. So, stocks are an asset class, bonds are an asset class, real estate is an asset class, and so on. At this point, you might be thinking this study is just stating the obvious when it reveals that the asset class we invest into determines growth. But remember, an inordinate amount of effort is constantly attempting to persuade you otherwise. Many in the investment industry would have you think that market timing and superior investment selection are the greatest determinants of growth.

The study further concludes that individual investment selection within an asset class makes little difference in the investment outcome. We discussed previously the illusions that superior, individual investment selection is not a viable means to achieving investment success. It is not whether you own stock in Costco or Coca-Cola that really determines long-term investment returns—it's whether you are invested in stocks versus bonds versus real estate that really makes the significant difference. It is the asset class selection that is almost exclusively responsible for determining long term performance.

1. Brinson, Gary P; Hood, L. Randolph; Beebower, Gilbert L. *Financial Analyst Journal.* July/August 1986.

Every investor, or for that matter, every investment portfolio, should have an asset allocation plan designed to meet the goals unique to that portfolio. Once an investment goal is determined, an asset allocation plan can be implemented. For example, if you were saving money toward purchasing a car next year, you would allocate your money differently than if you were investing money toward your retirement twenty years in the future. A proper asset allocation plan is a plan that matches your future income needs with your current investment portfolio.

Every asset class has its own set of positive and negative characteristics that must be recognized before attempting to create an asset allocation plan. For example, investing into equities has proven to be one of the highest returning asset classes in the long run, but equities are subject to volatility and are unreliable in the short term. Fixed-income investments such as bonds and money market instruments typically insulate investments from volatility but will surely be subject to the loss of purchasing power because of inflation. Real estate is usually found to be a good hedge against inflation, but like equities, real estate suffers from occasional bouts of volatility as well as issues with liquidity. The key is to understand the pros and cons of the various asset classes, and then create a portfolio of investments that fulfills your objectives with the least amount of risk.

When deciding how to allocate your investments, three questions must be answered:

- How long will my money be invested?
- How should I properly diversify?
- How much risk am I willing to take?

Because asset allocation is such an overwhelming determinant of the growth of your investments, the next three chapters are dedicated to taking a closer look at these questions.

Additionally, I would be remiss if I did not share with you the impact fees have on an investment portfolio. Fees are also a huge determinant of investment outcomes. Therefore, this section of the book will include a chapter to this often-overlooked determinant of growth.

CHAPTER 11

Time Horizon

"The big money is not in the buying and the selling, but in the sitting."

—Jesse Livermore

To adequately understand time horizon and how it affects the growth of your money, you need to understand compound interest and its importance. Compound interest is when an investment earns interest, on top of interest, on top of interest, and so on. When asked to name the greatest invention in human history, Albert Einstein simply replied, "compound interest." I likewise am impressed by compound interest; it's almost magical. Those who figure out how to harness the power of compound interest are wealthy. Those who are in debt, and allow this power to work against them, are forever poor.

THE LAW OF 72

The two components that drive compound interest are time and the rate of return on the investment. A simple math calculation reveals how compound interest works. I have heard this calculation referred to as the Law of 72.

Here is how it operates. Divide the number 72 by whatever rate of return you expect to get on an investment, and the quotient tells you how many years it will take your money to double in value. For example, if I were to expect a 5% return on my $10,000 investment, then I would divide 72 by 5, which tells me that my $10,000 would double to $20,000 in 14.4 years. Using this same formula, we find that money getting a 10% return doubles every 7.2 years. None of this information may seem that spectacular until you look at the results over a long period of time.

THE LAW OF 72

At a return rate of 4.8%— 72 divided by 4.8 = 15 years to double	
Year 1	$100,000
Year 15	$200,000
Year 30	$400,000

At a return rate of 9.6%— 72 divided by 9.6 = 7.5 years to double	
Year 1	$100,000
Year 7.5	$200,000
Year 15	$400,000
Year 22.5	$800,000
Year 30	$1,600,000

As you can see from the chart, the results of compound interest are truly fascinating. A $100,000 investment getting 4.8% over thirty years has the chance to double twice, allowing it to grow to $400,000. Whereas the investment that gets twice that return (9.6%) will be able to double four times, allowing that initial $100,000 investment to grow to $1,600,000 in thirty years. Thanks to compound interest, an investment that gets a 9.6% return versus a 4.8% return doesn't give you twice as much money in thirty years; it gives you four times as much money in thirty years!

When compound interest was introduced to me, it changed my life. I am approaching age sixty and I can tell you that compound interest really works. I have lived and taught the Law of 72 over my career, and countless people have been blessed by understanding and implementing it in their own lives. My own family has especially been blessed. Share the Law of 72 with someone you love, especially someone who is young enough to really put it to work in their own lives. They will forever be thankful to you.

INVESTMENT DURATION

When we talk about time horizon, we are simply seeking the answer to the question, "How long can my money stay invested?" Ascertaining a portfolio's time horizon is the single most important determination that must be decided before investing. According to Ibbotson,[1] since 1926, ultra-safe treasury bills have averaged an annualized return of 3.4%. Long-term government bonds have averaged 5.5% annually, and large U.S. stocks (the S&P 500) have had an average rate of return of 10% on an annualized basis. Therefore, a single dollar invested into treasury bills would be worth $21 today, a dollar invested into long-term government bonds would be worth $134 today, and a dollar invested into large U.S. stocks would be worth $6,035 today. Thank you, compound interest!

Sometimes, factual statements that lack additional insights can be misleading and lead to false expectations. If I were to end my explanation of historical stock market returns with the previous paragraph, I, too, would be guilty of misleading you because the information does not accurately portray the true nature of how equities grow. I am reminded of the infamous Inspector Clouseau in the *Pink Panther* movies. While the inspector was checking into a hotel, he asked the clerk if his dog bites. The clerk responded, "No, my dog doesn't bite." After hearing that, Inspector Clouseau reached down to pet the dog sitting at the clerk's feet, and the dog subsequently bit him. An angry Inspector Clouseau cried, "I thought you told me your dog doesn't bite!" The clerk calmly replied,

1. Ibbotson, Roger. 2017 SBBI Yearbook. 2–4

"*My* dog doesn't bite, that's not my dog." The clerk gave factual information, but it wasn't useful information, and it mislead Inspector Clouseau. So, to help you avoid getting bitten, let me clear up a few things.

TIME IN THE MARKET

Although the S&P 500 averaged a 10% return over the years, the history of U.S. equities from 1926 to the present is fraught with huge downturns, as well as incredible rallies, that cause even the most stoic investors occasional bouts of insomnia. This 10% average return has overcome multiple bear markets. In fact, more than a quarter of the years since 1926 have posted negative returns.

But there have also been tremendous periods of growth. After all is said and done, large U.S. equities have averaged an annualized return of 10%. So, it is true that equities over time are generally your best opportunity, but in the short term, (less than five years) investing in equities is a gamble. Nobody can predict the short-term direction of the stock market. Those who invest dollars into equities that will be needed in the short term, are often disappointed. **Don't invest short-term money into long-term investments!**

Because of the volatile nature of the stock market, some investors mistakenly avoid this lucrative class of investment altogether. Avoiding equities has proven, and will likely continue to prove, to be a monumental mistake. As I have mentioned previously, if you want your money to keep up with inflation, you must invest a portion of your money into equities. There is just no way around it. But how does one manage this manic-depressive business partner we call the stock market?

This question is best answered through an analogy. The headwaters of the Colorado River start high in the Rocky Mountains of Colorado and Wyoming. Annual runoff from the melting snowpack provides almost 90% of the water that flows into this valuable resource. The water provided by the Colorado River is the lifesaving supply that makes it possible for its 41 million thirsty users downstream to live in the arid southwestern United States. Indeed, the great cities of Phoenix, Las Vegas, and Los Angeles would not exist without this great river.

Prior to being tamed, the Colorado River was an erratic and undependable source of water, with extremes like no other river in the United States. The average flow of its water on an annual basis ran about 100,000 cubic feet per second during the spring of each year, and decreased to a mere 2,500 cubic feet per second during the winter months. Again, this was the average flow. The extremes, however, were mind-blowing. In 1884, the river was measured to have peaked at a whopping flow of 384,000 cubic feet per second. Cities along the river were wiped out during this extreme runoff. The smallest flow in recorded history occurred in 1935, when the river eked out a trickle of only 422 cubic feet per second.

So how can such a volatile and unpredictable resource be managed? Over time, twenty-nine dams were built on the various rivers that feed the Colorado, as well as some major dams that have been built on the Colorado River itself. The reservoirs created by these dams have the capacity to store four times the average annual water flow of the Colorado River. This vast system of dams controls flooding concerns, as well as stores water for the inevitable drought years, and even drought decades, that are so common in the desert southwest.

Like the Colorado River, stock market returns are not predictable and cannot accurately be forecasted. Volatility is the norm. The best single year for large U.S. stocks since 1925 was 54% and the worst single year for large U.S. stocks was -43%. The Colorado River drainage has a series of dams that control and level the flow of the river, so you might be asking, "Where are the dams that level out the erratic flow of the stock market?" The answer? Time. That's right—no expensive dams or complicated products need to be created. We simply must remember during the all-too-frequent stock market corrections that come our way, that the key to not being impacted by the volatility of the stock market is time and patience.

Since 1926, if you had invested into large U.S. stocks on the first day of each month and sold on the last day of each month, you would have had a positive return 62% of the time. If you had invested into large U.S. stocks on the first day of the year and sold on the last day of each year, you would have made money during 73% of those years. If you had invested each year and held your investment for a five-year period, you would have made money in 86% of those five-year periods. If you would have bought each year and held onto your stocks for a ten-year period, you would have made money in 95% of those ten-year periods. There has

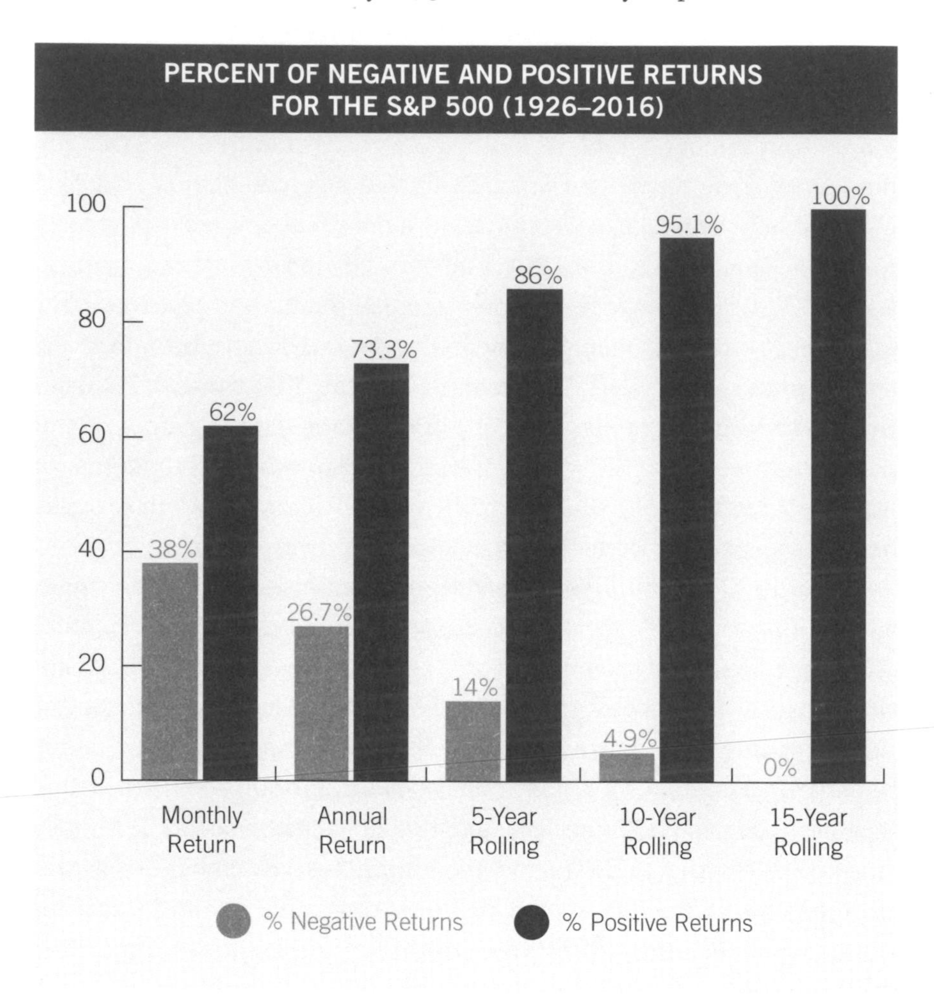

never been a fifteen-year period when you would not have made money buying and holding a diversified portfolio of large U.S. stocks.

It should be apparent that the less time you allow your money to be invested in equities, the more risk of loss you have. I don't recommend investing in equities for money that is needed within five years. Money that will be needed in the five-to-ten-year range could be invested into equities with a minimal risk of loss. Money not needed for ten years and beyond must be invested in equities if maintaining purchasing power is the objective. Remember, it's not timing the market, it's time *in* the market that counts.

Seasoned investors think in terms of decades when it comes to owning equities. Misguided day traders think in the terms of minutes when they purchase equities. There is a big difference between being a long-term investor and a short-term gambler. The average holding period of the purchasers of mutual funds is only about three years. It's no wonder there are so many disgruntled investors. Investing short-term dollars into long-term products is a game of chance and is not a prudent course of action, but many people are convinced that's how equities should be managed. I am continually amazed at the ingenuity of the average investor. They seem to always come up with new and exciting ways to lose money.

To help you understand the healing power of time, I would like to introduce you to two imaginary investors, Mr. Perfect and Mr. Pitiful. Both Mr. Perfect and Mr. Pitiful invested $10,000 annually for the last thirty years into the S&P 500 index, and reinvested their dividends. Mr. Perfect happened to invest his $10,000 on the best investment day of each year, when the stock market was at its lowest point. Mr. Pitiful, on the other hand, invested his $10,000 each year on the worst day of the year, when the markets were at their highest point. In other words, one of these gentlemen had perfect timing, and the other had the worst possible timing.

So, what were the results? Mr. Perfect accumulated $1,624,770 over the thirty years, averaging a 9.6% rate of return. Miraculously, Mr. Pitiful did quite well for himself, too. He accumulated $1,270,899, averaging 8.51% on his investment. In the end, their annualized rates of return were separated by a mere 1.09%. Certainly, we would all like to be Mr. Perfect, but, as previously discussed, timing the market is impossible. But being Mr. Pitiful ends up not being so bad, if you allow time to work in your behalf.

I am not a professor or a professional researcher. I manage investments for real people, through all market conditions. I can't ignore the mental anguish that so often accompanies market corrections. During a bear market, you wouldn't be human if you didn't feel the overwhelming urge to pull your money out of equities and bury the diminished remains of your portfolio into a bank account. It's difficult when you see your portfolio decrease by 20, 30, or even 40% during a market correction, but you can't allow yourself to lock in your losses. Stock market downturns are always temporary, and historically the average bear market decline has lasted less than two years. Bear markets are always followed by bull markets, and time is the great equalizer. Time allows even the unluckiest of investors to benefit from owning shares of the best-managed, most profitable corporations the world has ever known.

You need to develop a long-term commitment to equities in this short-term world in which we live. You need to develop a plan. A plan that protects your income from the volatility associated with equities, while, at the same time, protects your long-term investments from the ravages of inflation. A well-thought-out retirement income plan will mitigate many of the worries that accompany owning equities. Such a plan will be addressed in the later chapters of this book.

CHAPTER 12

DIVERSIFICATION

"The beauty of diversification is it's about as close as you can get to a free lunch in investing."

—Barry Ritholtz

Diversification is the second component of asset allocation.

Since the beginning of time, diversification of assets has been taught and practiced. The Bible, the Talmud, and even William Shakespeare left us words of wisdom regarding the importance of diversifying assets among various types of investments.

A simple example of the importance of diversification can be learned from the early Greeks. When they needed a harvest of grain shipped to a faraway port, they would divide the harvest amongst various ships. They would then send those ships to the destination by different trade routes, and at different times of the year, so if a single ship were lost at sea, the entire harvest of grain would not be lost. We can learn a lot from this simple example of diversification.

Diversification is the process of dividing your assets into various types of investments to have a safer and less volatile investment experience. In a diversified portfolio, you won't be hitting home runs, but you won't be striking out either. In retirement, the objective should not be to invest to become wealthy; the objective is to invest to stay wealthy. That's why we diversify.

I've seen the process of diversification likened to making salsa.[1] Good salsa has many ingredients: tomatoes, peppers, onions, cilantro, lime, etc. The correct combination of these ingredients results in the desired salsa. But everyone has their individual salsa preferences. Some like their salsa hot, some prefer a milder taste; some like it chunky, some like it puréed. My point is that an individualized salsa can be created through the proper mix of salsa ingredients.

Like salsa, combining the correct investments will result in the desired results within an individual's personal asset allocation model. The ingredients that make up an investment portfolio's asset allocation are the asset classes we discussed in the previous chapter. Therefore, the asset classes of stocks, bonds, real estate, commodities, and cash are the basic ingredients available to the investor to create the desired results.

Warning: These ingredients must be combined skillfully and in the right proportions for the desired outcomes to be achieved. Many mistakes are made by those that don't understand the need to diversify, or don't know the way to properly diversify investment portfolios.

NON-CORRELATED ASSETS

Diversification isn't about owning everything; it's about owning things that are opposites. It's about owning things that are not correlated to each other. Correlation refers to the strength of the linear relationship between two random variables. When two variables move perfectly in sync with each other, it is referred to as a +1 correlation. When they move

1. Craig L. Israelsen, *7Twelve: A Diversified Investment Portfolio with a Plan*, pg. 37.

exactly opposite of each other, it is referred to as a -1 correlation. When there is a 50% chance of each variable moving in either direction at any time, the variables have no correlation.

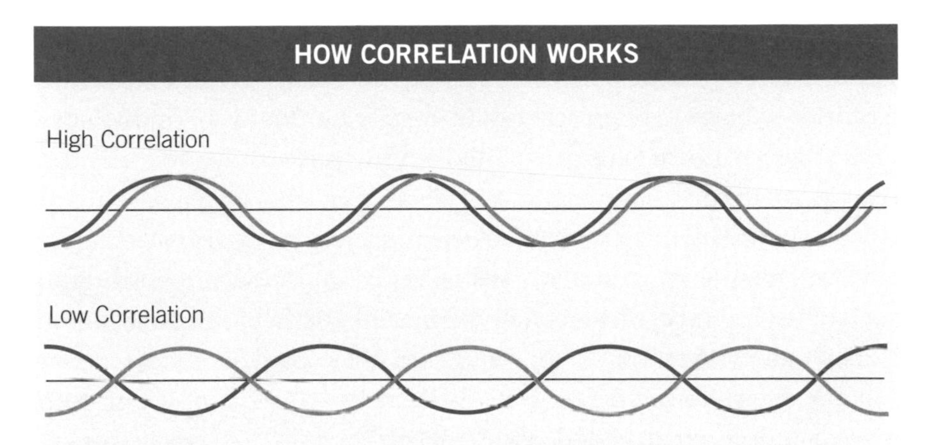

These diagrams are for illustrative purposes only and do not represent the correlation of any actual securities or index.

In a low-correlated investment portfolio, some of your investments will soar, while at the same time, other parts of your portfolio will bleed. Then, without warning, they will do a role reversal. That's what non-correlated asset classes tend to do.

For example, if equities were to experience a dramatic downturn on a given day, the bond portion of the portfolio may soar, or might be flat, depending on what the correlation of the stock and bond portfolios are to each other. If an investment portfolio only consists of highly correlated investments, when market and economic conditions worsen, the entire portfolio will take a hit. Adding low or non-correlated assets to the portfolio can help to mitigate this risk.

There are examples of low correlation all around us. Think about the "snowbird retirees," or the retirees that migrate south for the winter. They have a winter home in a desert climate to live in during the cold months of the year, and a home—or a mountain cabin—at higher elevations, where they can cool off during the heat of the summer. The benefit of owning both properties is that they have a negative correlation to one another.

I live in the mountains of Utah, and I have noticed that most landscaping companies also specialize in snow removal during the winter months, when landscaping is not happening. This is another situation where the benefits of recognizing the need for low correlation of resources pays off. Historically, commodities, real estate, bonds, and equities—both domestic and international—have exhibited a history of positive and negative correlation to each other.

In most cases, it is impossible to achieve a perfectly negative correlation, meaning that investments will never move in exact opposition to each other. However, a negatively correlated portfolio can be achieved through diversification of assets across these various asset classes. Historically, a low-correlated investment portfolio will begin with investments in equities and bonds. While equities have earned more throughout history, bonds have moved independently of equities. This combination of asset classes offers a hedge against the volatility associated with the stock market, and against the erosion of purchasing power associated with the bond market.

Of course, past performance is not an indicator of future results, but a wide range of investments with a low correlation have never crashed simultaneously. No one can predict market performance, but the study of correlations shows that, over time, the different asset classes have varying degrees of correlation to one another. A well-diversified and low-correlated portfolio has the objective of delivering the benefits of higher returns while experiencing less volatility.

DIVERSIFICATION MISCUES

In my day-to-day practice of managing money, I have come across a wide variety of misconceptions and mistakes regarding diversification. Most people understand the benefits, but very few seem to be able to properly diversify.

Under-Diversifying

It is not uncommon to run into a loyal employee of a large corporation who became wealthy by participating in their company's stock purchase plan. The result is that large percentages of the employee's retirement assets are tied to the success of a single company, and the price of the employer's stock. Over thirty years, I have heard the same story repeated time and time again. "I am wealthy because of my company stock, and besides, what could possibly happen to ExxonMobil, Citigroup, or Zions Bank . . . ?"

Now with 20/20 hindsight I can share with you what did happen to their stock. In 1989, Exxon stock plummeted when the Exxon Valdez ran ashore in the Gulf of Alaska, creating an environmental nightmare that cost Exxon billions of dollars in cleanup and fines. Both Citigroup's as well Zions Bank's stocks dropped precipitously in the financial crisis of 2008–09, and have never recovered. Several pharmaceutical companies have gone out of existence, or merged with other companies when their stock crashed, because the FDA failed to approve the drug they were hoping to bring to market.

What I am trying to share is that it is dangerous to have all your eggs in the same basket. Much of the risk associated with owning equities can be swept away through diversification. Individual stocks come and go, but the entire U.S. economy will not go away. The overall economy will surely have its ups and downs, but it will never go out of business and has proven to be quite resilient. Investors who had all their money concentrated into the former financial powerhouse companies such as Pan Am, Kodak, Enron, and Lehman Brothers can share with you the sad tale of the devastation that occurs by not being sufficiently diversified.

Redundancy

The best way I can illustrate the problem of redundancy is to introduce you to my friend Mack, and the decisions he made regarding diversification.

Mack had a successful business that he sold for a significant sum of money. He had read about the importance of having a diversified portfolio, so he decided on a plan to ultra-diversify his investments. Mack hired three different financial advisors to manage his wealth. He instructed each of his advisors the same way, as to what the goals were for his money. He told them of the positive experience he had previously, of owning shares of large U.S. stocks. Mack assumed each of his advisors would suggest different kinds of investments and have different biases, and they did. One advisor worked for Merrill Lynch and invested Mack's money into a variety of Merrill Lynch's mutual funds. The next advisor worked for Fidelity and invested his portion into the best Fidelity funds. The last advisor was an independent registered investment advisor (RIA),[2] and set Mack up with some low-cost Vanguard mutual funds, exchange-traded funds (ETFs), and a portfolio of individual shares of stocks in large U.S. corporations. When all the money was invested, Mack owned sixty different mutual funds and ETFs and almost 100 different stocks.

Getting back to the analogy of the salsa, Mack thought he had created a wonderful salsa of investments with all the different advisors and products he had included in his portfolio. What Mack didn't understand was that all his advisors put him into mutual funds and ETFs that contained the same large U.S. stocks. That's right—the mutual fund managers at Merrill Lynch, Fidelity, and Vanguard all loaded up on the same stocks within their respective mutual funds, stocks that were highly correlated and that moved in tandem. Besides owning individual shares of Apple, Boeing, ExxonMobil, Coca-Cola, and many other individual shares of stock, these same companies were all found in the mutual funds and ETFs Mack owned.

After analyzing Mack's portfolio, it was discovered that 93% of his portfolio was highly correlated. He was investing almost entirely in large U.S. stock companies. Mack hadn't created a diversified salsa of investments; he had created a very expensive collection of tomatoes. Owning dozens of mutual funds that all hold the same underlying investments in the same asset class is not diversifying; it's duplicating. Remember that diversification happens when asset classes are combined, not individual

2. A registered investment advisor (RIA) is an investment advisor who charges a fee for investment management, instead of receiving a commission on transactions, as most brokers do. RIAs are independent investment management entities that are not usually affiliated with large institutional brokerage firms.

securities. A truly diversified, non-correlated portfolio would include international, emerging market, large, small, as well as mid-size company stocks. It would have some real estate, U.S. and international bonds, and possibly some commodities.

After understanding what he had created, Mack made some changes. He went from owning 160 different investments to owning eleven. Not only is his reconstituted portfolio easier to manage and significantly cheaper than his previous portfolio, but it is also much less correlated. An excellent salsa was created.

DIVERSIFICATION: AN ONGOING PROCESS

Diversification is not a once-and-done exercise. It requires vigilance to stay diversified as investments go up and down in value within a portfolio. Once the proper mix of investments is determined for your unique situation, you should maintain that mix of investments.

The process of returning a portfolio of investments back to its original allocation is called rebalancing. Rebalancing is a counterintuitive process, and at first glance doesn't make sense because it requires that you sell the best-performing part of your portfolio on occasion and use the proceeds to purchase more of the worst-performing part of your portfolio. But when you understand the frequent role reversals of the various asset classes, rebalancing makes sense.

Whether you rebalance monthly, quarterly, or annually, it is not nearly as important as making sure you regularly rebalance. I choose to rebalance my personal investment portfolio annually, on my wedding anniversary, because it's an easy day to remember. This makes August 7 of each year a red-letter day for me. Remembering my anniversary keeps me from sleeping on the couch; remembering to rebalance my portfolio ensures I will always have a couch to sleep on.

Diversification makes sense to most investors, but few investors do it well. Creating an asset allocation plan, determining an appropriate investment mix, and adhering to that mix through systematic rebalancing are all keys to maintaining a well-diversified investment program.

CHAPTER 13

RISK PROPENSITY

"Investing should be more like watching paint dry or watching grass grow. If you want excitement, take $800 and go to Vegas."

—Paul Samuelson

After time horizon and diversification are considered, the third and final consideration of an asset allocation plan should be the investor's propensity for risk. The first two tenets of asset allocation go a long way toward reducing investment risk. In fact, almost all risks associated with investing can be mitigated through diversification and patience.

In Chapter 10, I described exactly what risk isn't. Remember, risk is not volatility. Volatility itself does not lead to poor long-term performance, rather it is the emotional reaction to volatility that ultimately leads to poor performance.

So, we know what risk isn't. Let's answer the question of what risk is. Financially speaking, risk is the loss of purchasing power. Sometimes, purchasing power is lost in dramatic fashion, like when a business fails. Other times, the erosion of purchasing power is so gradual that the loss of purchasing power is imperceptible, such as in the case of inflation.

Every asset class is susceptible to its unique set of risks. Bonds are victims to interest rates, default, and inflation risks. Real estate has liquidity and market risks. Equities and commodities likewise have market risks to deal with. Fixed annuities and bank deposits are subject to inflation risks. All of these risks can erode purchasing power.

Many investors tend to either ignore the risks of their situation, or they don't understand the risks that have the greatest potential to inflict damage. When I think of risks, I think of my personal phobia of sharks. I can't think of anything more frightening than being attacked by a shark. My fear is shared by millions. In fact, there are many people who are so afraid of sharks they refuse to even get into the ocean. I have done research on the frequency of shark attacks, and surprisingly discovered that of the more than seven billion people that populate the planet, on average, only ten people per year die from shark attacks. Ten. That means I have only a one in 728 million chance of dying of a shark attack. I would say my chances are pretty good that I won't be dying of a shark attack any time soon. On the other hand, 66,000 people die from skin cancer each year. That means I have a one in 110,000 chance of dying from skin cancer. I am 6,600 times more likely to die from skin cancer than a shark attack!

It appears that, when I go to the beach, my fellow shark phobics and I are worrying about the wrong kind of risk. It's not the dramatic, sudden shark attack that will kill us; it's being exposed to the sun that is more likely to do us in. So, it is with investments. The dramatic but temporary declines in the stock market, though scary, don't do near as much damage as does the day-to-day loss of purchasing power caused by inflation. That is why it's important to understand all the risks in your own situation and do what you can to minimize them.

EMOTIONAL RISK

When you really drill down, you will find that investment decisions driven by emotion are at the core of almost all investment losses. Ironically, the investors themselves are likely the most dangerous risk their own portfolios will ever face. Humans are naturally horrible investors, because the act of investing is counterintuitive to our very nature. For example, selling our best-performing investments and regularly buying underperforming investments to rebalance our portfolios is a prudent, yet perplexing exercise. Buying equities when the rest of the world is selling, or selling when everybody else is buying, is likewise a productive, yet counterintuitive, practice. Few investors can demonstrate this level of investment prowess.

The cartoon character Pogo Possum perhaps said it best when he once described his situation: "We have met the enemy, and he is us." Pogo Possum is not alone in this assessment. Look at what some of the greatest investors in history have to say about the emotionally driven investor:

"Individuals who cannot master their emotions are ill-suited to profit from the investment process." —*Benjamin Graham*

"The biggest investing errors come not from factors that are informational or analytical, but from those that are psychological." —*Howard Marks*

"Until you can manage your emotions, don't expect to manage money." —*Warren Buffett*

"Wealth isn't primarily determined by investment performance, but by investor behavior." —*Nick Murray*

As you can see from the following chart, if investors would have selected any asset class and stuck with it, they would have outperformed what the average investor was able to generate over the last twenty years. Unfortunately, it looks as if Pogo Possum was right.

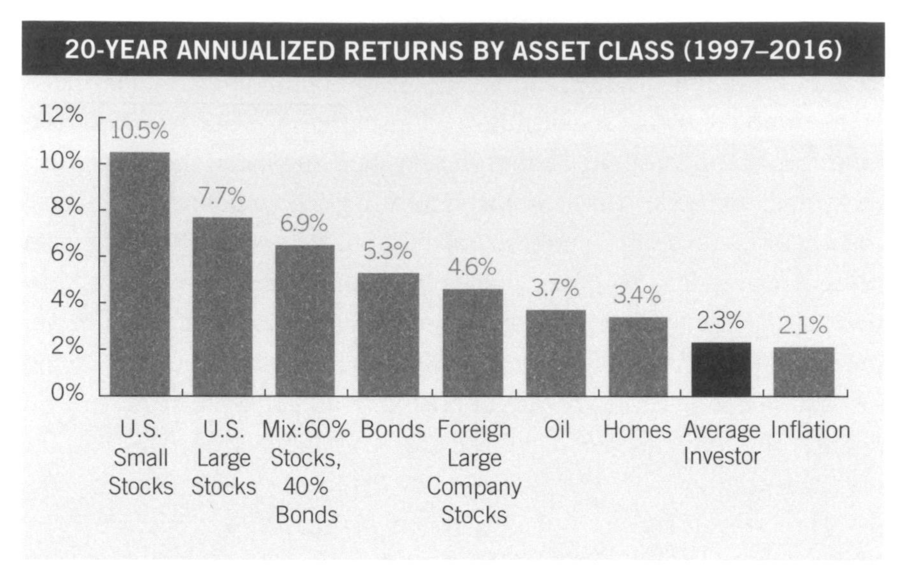

Source: J.P. Morgan, *Guide to the Markets* as of June 30, 2017, pg. 63.

For over three decades of investment management, I have seen investors destroy perfectly designed investment programs because of something they saw on the internet, or because somebody they overheard at church or work has voiced an opinion that stocks are about to crash. In my office, we refer to the creation and subsequent destruction of a well-thought-out asset allocation plan as "rearranging the deck chairs on the *Titanic*."

Let me illustrate some prevalent instances of "deck-chair rearranging" I often see. I share these common blunders in hopes that you won't get caught up in these same destructive practices. As you will see, unsuccessful investors are swayed by current events, they lack discipline, and are driven by emotion. Their own behavior is indeed their greatest risk.

THE RISK OF MAKING DECISIONS BASED ON POLITICS

I live in one of the most politically conservative counties, in the most politically conservative state, in America. During the Obama presidency, I constantly heard that life as we knew it was over and that the stock market was going to collapse under the crushing debt caused by the cost of the social programs introduced by President Obama. I would hear people say, "The man is a socialist who hates our country, and he probably wasn't even born in the United States, which renders him ineligible to even be the president and there is no way investments can prosper with him at the helm."

Because I have clients spread throughout the United States, I was also privy to a different flavor of despair when President Trump was elected. I have heard him called a "fascist like Adolf Hitler." I have heard people say, "he is in office only because the Russians conspired with him to steal the Presidency. He and his billionaire buddies will stop at nothing to enrich themselves at the expense of the American people. Never has there been such an amateur in the White House. Certainly, no thoughtful investor would risk investing during the Trump regime."

History has proven both extremes to be horribly wrong. During the Obama era, the stock market surged 235% while we enjoyed one of the longest-running bull markets in the history of the United States. Since the day Donald Trump was elected, the equities markets have taken off like a rocket. The various U.S. equities markets are all in record territory.

The reality is that profits ultimately drive the equities markets, not politics. The corporations that make up the stock markets are more efficient and profitable than ever. The creators of the iPhone, and the engineers that developed the technology behind horizontal drilling and fracking, have had a greater impact on our day-to-day lives than any politician ever could have. Betting against the entrepreneurial drive of the American people to improve life has always been a loser's game, no matter what your political leanings might be and no matter who occupies the White House.

Once again, Warren Buffett, the most admired and least followed investor of our time, can serve as our example. Buffett was a major contributor to the Hillary Clinton campaign. When Secretary Clinton lost the election to Donald Trump, Buffett did not liquidate his investments. He stayed invested, and to date, his portfolio of investments has grown by $10 billion since the candidate he did not support won the election. He didn't let the political climate dictate his investment decisions, and he was rewarded handsomely.

THE RISK OF GREED

"Bulls make money, bears make money, pigs get slaughtered" is an old Wall Street maxim. In other words, optimists do well, pessimists do well, but the greedy never do well when it comes to investing. Although I disagree that being a pessimist is a moneymaker, I must concur that pigs do indeed get slaughtered.

The greedy, or "pigs," are investors whose goal is to make the most money in the shortest amount of time. Piggish investors are known to either take on high degrees of risk or overlook risk to make a profit. They often make rash decisions and invest without doing their due diligence. As a result, they inevitably lose money, hence the adage that they get slaughtered.

Chasing last year's top-performing investment and guessing the short-term direction of equities markets are a favorite pastime of pigs. The excitement of making a quick buck replaces the tried-and-true investment virtues of discipline and patience. They ignore the value of long-term investing as well as the benefits of diversification.

The greedy take safe, dependable, long-term investment tools, such as the equity or real-estate markets, and attempt to use them as short-term gambling instruments. They use good tools in the wrong way. Just as we shouldn't use a hammer to tighten a screw or a wrench to drive a nail, we shouldn't use long-term investments for short-term speculation.

THE RISK OF FEAR

Fear, the opposite emotion of greed, inflicts its own brand of investment-destroying damage. This paralyzing emotion likewise causes the investor to misuse legitimate investment tools. Fear causes the investor to use short-term investment tools, such as bank deposits and bonds, as long-term investment solutions. Mistaking volatility for risk and, in turn, focusing on ensuring that their investment will never go down, is the calling card of the fearful. The fearful are either ignorant or apathetic to the risk of inflation. They are content with virtually no return on their investment as long as they don't ever see their account balance go down.

Peter Lynch said, "Far more money has been lost by investors preparing for corrections, or trying to anticipate corrections, than has been lost in corrections themselves." Think about this. Investors are more than willing to systematically watch their purchasing power erode, because they are afraid of the pain associated with a temporary stock market correction. They are willing to pay unbelievably high fees to insurance companies that sell annuities and that promise to protect their money should the market crash. Some investors willingly throw money at the poorest of investments and subject their money to the promises of the shadiest of characters before they allow their money to be exposed to the temporary fluctuation in price of a share of the most profitable companies the world has ever known. The fearful investors are so focused on missing the next bear market that they willingly skip out on one of the most profitable investment opportunities ever made available to mankind: investing in equities.

As mentioned previously, the price of inflation-beating returns is enduring volatility. Certainly, there will be temporary periods of pain and discomfort from investing into equities, but the pain of owning a well-diversified portfolio of equities has always proven to be temporary, and the long-term results have always been able to protect purchasing power. I have always been curious about why we humans willingly subject ourselves to the temporary discomfort and sometimes outright pain of going to the doctor or dentist when we know in advance that our visit will be uncomfortable, but we are not willing to subject ourselves to occasional, temporary discomfort in our investments to inoculate our investments from the erosion of purchasing power.

Investing is more of an emotional exercise than it is intellectual. Those who can harness their emotions will be successful. Those who lack the emotional maturity to be a disciplined investor will struggle. Every investor needs to have an investment goal in mind, and then create an asset allocation plan with the objective to achieve that desired goal. Without a goal-driven plan, emotions drive our investment decisions. And *emotionally* charged investing will never produce a good investment outcome.

CHAPTER 14

FEES

"Price is what you pay. Value is what you get."

—*Warren Buffett*

The Brinson, Hood, and Beebower study, which I referred to at the beginning of this section, established that asset allocation was largely responsible for the growth of investments. But its research was done without considering the impact fees have on the growth of an investment portfolio. Because of the tremendous influence fees have on investment outcomes, a discussion about them needs to take place.

Most investors understand that all investments have fees, but few realize the huge disparity that exists among investment fees. The lack of transparency, or the difficulty the average investor has with uncovering the fees associated with their investments, adds to the confusion surrounding fees.

Fees are assessed differently for almost every investment product. There are fees to buy, fees to sell, ongoing management fees, transaction fees, marketing fees, and a myriad of other fees that take away from your bottom line.

Make no mistake about it. All investments have fees. Yes, your 401(k), annuity, and mutual funds all have fees. Just because you can't see the fees you are paying doesn't mean the fees don't exist. And unfortunately, the fees you can't readily see are usually the most expensive. I find that most investors really don't know the fees they pay on their investments, so they subsequently underestimate the impact fees have on a portfolio.

Fees are a necessary component of the investment process. Of course, people who create investment products for us to invest our money into, those that spend their careers doing investment research and analyses in our behalf, and even your local investment advisor all need to be compensated. The key is to know the fees you are paying, and to make sure that what you are paying is reasonable.

I like to think of fees this way. If you were to have two horses in a race, which horse would likely win the race—the horse with the 120-pound jockey, or the horse with the 240-pound jockey?

Of course, there is a chance that the horse with the heavier jockey might win an occasional race, but the vast majority of the time, the horse with the lighter jockey will win. So it is with investments. The least expensive investments typically win out. Therefore, fees should always be taken into consideration when selecting investments.

TYPES OF INVESTMENTS AND THEIR ASSOCIATED FEES

Exchange-Traded Funds

Exchange-traded funds (ETFs) are the most economical way that I have found to invest into a diversified portfolio of investments. An ETF is a security designed to mimic an index. There are ETFs that will track a stock index, a bond index, commodities index, and so forth. Because of their index-tracking approach to investing, ETFs are naturally cheaper than other investment vehicles. According to the *Wall Street Journal*,[1] the average cost of an ETF is .44%. This fee is less expensive than what mutual funds charge, making the ETFs the investment of choice for passive investors. They are the horses with the light-weight jockeys on the track.

Mutual Funds

Mutual funds have been the darlings of the investment industry for decades and are still the most popular way to invest into equities. (If you have a 401(k), you own a mutual fund.) In the beginning, mutual funds were a great concept, because they offered professional management at a low cost. Unfortunately, over the years, the mutual fund industry has figured out ways to exact more and more fees from the unwary investor. These extra charges render mutual funds, once the most economical way to purchase equities, to be not so economical anymore. The average expense ratio for a mutual fund is .64%, but buyer beware: expense ratios only tell part of the story. Account fees, transaction costs, purchase and redemption fees, and 12b-1 fees all add to the fee burden of a mutual fund.

1. How to Choose an Exchange-Traded Fund (ETF). The Wall Street Journal, December 17th, 2008 *<http://guidelines.wsj.com/personal-finance/investing/how-to-choose-an-exchange-traded-fund-etf>*.

According to the best resources[2] I have found, the average cost of owning a mutual fund is more than 2%, or almost five times the average cost of owning an ETF. If you are wondering about the fees you are paying in your own situation, check out *www.personalfunds.com.*

Variable Annuities

In Chapter 10, I introduced you to the index annuity. I now want to warn you of another popular, yet expensive, way to invest: the variable annuity.

Like the index annuity, variable annuities are investment products that are created by insurance companies and sold by insurance agents. Variable annuities in their different forms tend to be the most expensive way to purchase a portfolio of investments. In short, the underlying investments of the variable annuity are the same expensive mutual funds we discussed in the previous section. But this time, those expensive funds are purchased within an even more expensive insurance "wrapper."

The question that needs answering is, "Why would anyone purchase their already expensive mutual funds within an annuity, where even more expenses are added?" According to Forbes,[3] the average cost of a variable annuity is 3.1% annually. Besides the normal costs associated with these products, variable annuities usually offer a smorgasbord of optional benefits and guarantees—for an additional price. Insuring account values at the death of the owner and guaranteeing future income benefits from the variable annuity are the most prevalent guarantee riders that are offered.

These guarantee riders can be very expensive, and can make it almost impossible for an annuity to earn a reasonable return. It is not uncommon to find variable annuities loaded down with guarantee riders, which

---

2. Roger Edelen, Richard Evans, and Gregory Kadlec, "Shedding Light on 'Invisible' Costs: Trading Costs and Mutual Fund Performance," Financial Analysts Journal 69:1 (January 2013) 33-42.

Michael Rawson, "2015 Fee Study: Investors Are Driving Expense Ratios Down" (Chicago, IL. Morningstar, published report, 2015).

Katie Rushkewicz, "How Tax-Efficient Is Your Mutual Fund?" (Chicago, IL. Morningstar, published report, 2010).

3. Eve Kaplan, "Annuities: The Good, the Bad and the Ugly" July 15,2015. <*https://www.forbes.com/site/feeonlyplanner/2015/07/15/annuities-the-good-the-bad-and-the-ugly/#300fcaf27990*>.

assess the investor annual charges of 2–3% in addition to the already expensive fees that annuities charge. The insurance salespersons who sell annuities will undoubtedly proclaim all the virtues and guarantees associated with annuities. But in my estimation, and in almost every circumstance, there are better and less costly solutions for the average investor than annuities.

Again, "annuities are not bought; they are sold." Annuities are some of the highest commission-paying products in the investment universe, so it would make sense that they would come with high expenses. It is difficult to ascertain all the fees associated with annuities, and the quarterly statements sent to annuity owners don't reveal what the actual fees of the annuities are. Many investors incorrectly assume that because they never see the fees of their annuities, they must not exist. Wrong. The bottom line is, variable annuities cost too much.

As I speak of fees, please understand that I am speaking in general terms. There are exceptions to every rule when it comes to fees. Some ETFs are more expensive than some mutual funds. Annuities purchased through a fee-based (versus a commissioned-based) investment advisor can be quite economical. I am not suggesting that you never own an annuity or mutual fund. What I am saying is, know your fees and understand your investment products before you buy. Don't bet on a horse with a 300-pound jockey!

In this book, I have referred to the stock market frequently. I have been referring to the broad market, or the S&P 500. The S&P 500 is an index, or an unmanaged basket of stocks of the five hundred largest companies in the U.S. You can buy investments that mimic the S&P 500 index in the form of ETFs, mutual funds, and variable annuities.

To illustrate the impact that fees can have on your investment returns, let's compare what an investment into the S&P 500 index would be worth if one were to have invested 30 years ago into the least expensive product that mimics the S&P 500. Then, let's compare the results of investing in the most expensive product that mimics the S&P 500 index.

The cheapest way I could find to invest into the S&P 500 would be to purchase an ETF with a charge of .04%. The most expensive way to access the S&P 500 would be investing into a variable annuity with a charge of 2.57%. I chose not to share with you the names of the products that are the champs and the chumps of the fee contest because each year it changes.

An investment of $100,000 in 1987 into the low-cost ETF would have grown to $1,635,160 by 2017, whereas an investment in the variable annuity would have grown to only $812,329, or less than 50% of the low fee alternative. Both examples invested in exactly the same investments. The only difference between the two were the fees that were charged.

Getting back to our jockey analogy, the jockey in the cheap ETF that mimics the S&P 500 weighs a mere 4 pounds, while the more expensive form of purchasing the S&P 500 index, the variable annuity, weighs 257 pounds. In an effort to fully disclose, neither the inexpensive ETF nor the costly variable annuity were sold in 1987, so this comparison could not have happened, but they are both available to purchase today. Choose wisely, and know your fees!

THE COST OF USING A FINANCIAL ADVISOR

Are financial advisors worth the money you pay them? Or should you save the fee you would normally pay an advisor and invest on your own? My answer may surprise you. You need only a very good one. If your current advisor is telling you when to be in and out of the stock market, or is selecting a superior investment portfolio that will "beat the market," you need to fire that advisor. That kind of advisor will not only cost you unnecessarily, but could also do irreparable damage. If your advisor creates a plan for you and then helps you stick with that plan through all the inevitable gyrations of the economy and the markets, then your advisor is worth every dollar you pay them. Thank them, and cherish that relationship.

Many of you may not need a financial advisor currently if you are in the accumulation mode, or in other words, if you are still contributing to 401(k)s or IRAs. You might be able to oversee the investment management on your own, as long as you don't allow yourself to be scared out of equities when the occasional and inevitable bear market comes around.

If you question your ability or temperament to invest wisely, please seek the direction of a professional.

A good financial advisor is particularly valuable when the investor transitions from the accumulation mode to the distribution mode of investing at retirement. Coordinating a working career of accumulations into a stream of income that will last throughout retirement is a major challenge, and needs the oversight of a financial advisor who has developed a specialization in retirement income planning. Not only do the investments need to be carefully managed, but pensions and social security benefits also must be coordinated with investment income to maximize your overall retirement income. The goal is to create a stream of tax-efficient, inflation-beating income that will last for decades.

There is a specialized level of expertise that is required to manage an income stream through retirement. Be aware that, oftentimes, the investment advisor that helped you accumulate for retirement isn't necessarily the best advisor to guide you during the distribution stage. You need a retirement income planner, a professional that has developed a specialty in creating and maintaining retirement income streams, and who is capable of managing and coordinating your retirement income plan.

Just as you need to know the fees your investments have, you also need to know how your investment advisor is being compensated. Is the advisor compensated for selling you a product (commissioned based)? Or is the advisor compensated by charging you a fee on the amount of money they are managing for you (fee based)? If I were hiring an investment advisor to manage my family's wealth, I would consider the advisor as I would my employee. I would want a clear idea of exactly how I am paying this employee. I would want to know the methodology behind their investment selection. I would want clarity on the planned frequency of our contact, and I would want to know all the fees I would be paying, either through purchasing and owning a product or through direct compensation to the investment advisor.

If you can't get straight answers regarding all the fees you will need to pay, then it's best to move on to a new advisor. A little bit of homework will go a long way. If you choose to hire a financial advisor, you owe it to yourself and your family to find an experienced professional that shares your investment philosophy.

WHAT A FINANCIAL ADVISOR SHOULD DO FOR YOU

I would suggest that you look for a financial advisor that is compensated by charging a fee, rather than one who gets paid to sell a product. It is easy to ascertain how much you are paying a fee-based advisor, and there is less conflict of interest when investment products are selected on your behalf. The cost of using a fee-based advisor will usually be 1–1.5% annually of your investments under management with that advisor. For that compensation, the investment advisor fulfills three critical functions:

1. *The investment advisor creates financial, estate planning, and retirement income plans specific to you and your family's needs.*

These plans drive all the investment decisions. They need to be goal oriented, kept current, and reviewed at least annually. Changes to the plans should be implemented only when major life changes occur, or goals are altered.

2. *The investment advisor constructs an asset allocation plan, specific to your risk tolerance, time horizon, age, and income needs.*

The investment advisor then selects the investment products from amongst the thousands of mutual funds, ETFs, and a myriad of other investments that are best suited to accomplish your goals, with the least amount of risk and expense. The product selection should be determined based on the fee structure, the tax efficiency, and the experience and philosophy of those that manage the investment product. A properly diversified, non-correlated portfolio is then monitored, and occasionally adjusted as needed.

3. *The financial advisor saves you from your own destructive investment behavior.*

This is their most important function, whether it is to prevent you from liquidating all your equities when the stock market is down 30% or talking you out of buying that latest trend stock that has already gone up

200%. An educated, experienced, independent voice of reason is always important. A well-constructed, goal-driven retirement income plan will help you to have the discipline necessary to survive the volatile investment future you will occasionally experience. The highest and best function of a financial advisor, may simply be in convincing you to not give in to fear and sell. The decision not to sell will someday be the most important investment decision you will ever make.

Studies have shown[4] that those investors that have an advisor directing them, do better than those that invest on their own. I believe these studies to be true, but I can't stress enough the need to thoroughly vet any advisor that you hire to manage your finances.[5] Your advisor should be free of having any previous regulatory issues. Your advisor should share your same investment philosophy. Above all, your advisor must conduct your affairs with the upmost integrity. The bottom line is, that your financial advisor should care more about your money, than anyone who doesn't share your last name, and they should be experienced and competent dealing with retirement issues.

QUESTIONS TO ASK WHEN HIRING AN ADVISOR

In the appendix of this book I have provided a list of questions you can use as you interview potential candidates who are applying for the job of helping you to secure your financial future.

4. Francis M. Kinniry Jr., Colleen M. Jaconetti, Michael A. DiJoseph and Yan Zilbering, 2014. "Putting a Value on Your Value: Quantifying Vanguard Advisors Alpha." Valley Forge, Pa.: The Vanguard Group.

5. Before picking a financial advisor, check to see if they have had complaints or regulatory issues. You can do that by visiting these websites:
https://brokercheck.finra.org
https://adviserinfo.sec.gov/IAPD/Default.aspx

Step Six

Create a Retirement Income Plan

So it's finally your turn to retire. You contributed diligently for four decades into various retirement accounts. Your employer may have matched some of those contributions. You have saved, invested, and might have even been fortunate enough to have inherited a sum of money or sold a business along the way. You are now eligible to start receiving a Social Security and possibly a pension check. Congratulations on this wonderful accomplishment, you are now ready to retire!

Take a victory lap, but don't go too far. There is a lot of work to be done—the work of turning your lifetime of accumulations into a stream of inflation-beating income that will last the rest of your life.

The underlying question that needs to be answered by anyone considering retirement is, "Will I outlive my money, or will my money outlive me?" Longevity, inflation, your own investment management skills, as well as future economic conditions all factor into the success or failure of your financial future.

You will have to make critical decisions. You will have to answer difficult questions, questions you have probably never considered before:

- How much can I, or should I, withdraw from my retirement accounts?
- From which of my investments should I withdraw my future income?
- When should I start Social Security?
- How do I coordinate disbursements from retirement funds with my Social Security and pension payments to maximize my income and minimize my tax liability?
- How do I keep my money safe from the ravages of inflation but at the same time not lose money to stock market downturns?

These are just a sampling of the questions you will be faced with at and during retirement.

Thus far in this book, we have:

- Identified retirement challenges
- Discussed retirement readiness
- Debunked false investment concepts
- Described the true determinants of investment growth

These topics have prepared you for the final and essential step of creating a retirement income plan.

Having a plan is essential. As you read this book, you may be telling yourself that a plan isn't all that important because you have gotten through life without a plan thus far and everything has worked out well. Let me remind you, that once retired, the big earning years are over with. You will have to make do with the resources you have accumulated and the monthly income streams provided through pensions and Social Security. You won't have the time to recover from investment mistakes as you did during your working years. Mistakes made at or during retirement can be unforgiving; there are no do-overs. The quality of the next thirty years of your life are dependent upon the decisions that you now make and the plan that you now put into place. A well thought out plan will provide discipline, order and peace of mind and allow you to pursue your retirement dreams.

There are a couple of additional reasons for having a retirement income plan that may not have crossed your mind. New retirees are usually competent when it comes to financial decision-making. However, as I have worked with retirees over the last thirty years, I have seen that as we age, our financial decision-making abilities deteriorate. Even though you have endured many bear markets during your lifetime and not allowed yourself to give into panic, that doesn't mean you will be able to do the same when you are eighty or ninety.

What about your spouse? If you are the member of the family reading this book, chances are, your spouse depends on you as the designated money authority of the family. Who is going to help your spouse make prudent decisions when you slip from this life?

Because of the reality of impaired financial judgment as we age and the very real possibility that you will leave your less-than-financially-savvy spouse in charge of the family finances when you are gone, a plan is important. Having a retirement income plan will satisfy the need to have a plan in place to guide you in your older years as well as provide a foundation upon which your spouse can manage the family financial affairs after your death. The key is to create a plan while you are financially competent and then be disciplined enough to follow the plan throughout your retirement.

The balance of this book is dedicated to helping you to organize the various investments you have accumulated during your working lifetime. The goal is to organize your investments into a stream of inflation-adjusted income that will last the rest of your life.

CHAPTER 15

The Retirement Income Plan

> *"Every successful investor I have ever known was acting continuously on a plan. Every failed investor I've ever known was reacting continually to current events."*
>
> *—Nick Murray*

Before we start to create a retirement income plan, let's describe exactly what it is that we need a retirement income plan to accomplish. I believe a retirement income plan must achieve four objectives:

- Be goal-specific
- Create a framework for distribution
- Create a framework for investing
- Create a framework to reduce risk

1. A RETIREMENT INCOME PLAN MUST BE GOAL-SPECIFIC

A proper retirement income plan is goal-driven. It is a date-specific, dollar-specific blueprint that will guide you throughout retirement. A date-specific, dollar-specific plan defines how much money will be needed during retirement, and when it will be needed. Its objective is to deliver future dollars to the retiree with the least amount of risk. A properly structured retirement income plan matches your current investment strategy with your future income needs. Like any goal-driven program, the performance toward reaching the goal must be monitored to maintain discipline, and allow for adjustments if the goal is to be realized.

There is a big difference between a person who says, "When I retire, I would like to own a cabin at the lake," versus, "I want a cabin by the lake when I retire in twenty years. I estimate that it will cost $600,000. Therefore, I will need to save $1,300 per month for the next twenty years and get a 6% return on my investments to accomplish this goal." Clearly, the first statement is a wish or a dream; the second statement is a plan. Any program that does not offer specifics is a wish or dream, not a plan. In the world of finance, dreams rarely come true, but plans do.

Most retirees, as well as most investment advisors, manage investments without specific plans in mind. They are therefore managing wishes, not plans. Allow me to share with you the prevailing wishes of our day.

Wishing on Historical Averages

Here is a typical sales pitch about relying on historical averages: "Historically, equities have averaged over 10%, and bonds have averaged about 5%. Therefore, if you have 50% of your money invested in equities and 50% of your money invested in bonds, then you should average an annualized return of 7.5% on your investment portfolio. All you must do is withdraw 7% annually from your investments, or about .5% less than what you are earning, and all is well. As long as you rebalance your portfolio on occasion, to maintain the 50/50 mix of stocks versus bonds, you should do just fine during retirement. In fact, your retirement portfolio should actually grow a little."

Upon first glance, this method of providing retirement income from investments sounds appealing and makes sense. Unfortunately, this method of creating retirement income is deeply flawed. It just doesn't work.

The problem with projecting averages in a linear fashion is that the averages are derived from a series of numbers, both higher and lower than the average, which do not resemble the "average" very much. It is true that the S&P 500, or large U.S. stocks, have averaged a 10% annualized return, but rarely did the annual return come close to the 10% average. The majority of the years posted either negative returns or returns more than 20%. On an annual basis, the large stocks that produced the 10% average return have fluctuated from a high of 54% to a low of -43 %. Bonds likewise have truly averaged 5%, historically. We are currently in a rising interest rate environment, which is detrimental to bonds. The chance of getting a 5% return from investing in bonds is highly unlikely for the foreseeable future.

Projecting returns in a linear manner based on past averages is like deciding to wade across a river that is, on average, four feet deep. The average depth of the river may indeed be four feet deep, but that knowledge won't help you when you sink into a section of the river that is eight feet deep. In the same sense, taking a systematic withdrawal from an equities portfolio can blow up when the occasional down year, or even the occasional down decade, in the price of equities comes along. Planning retirement income based on projections of past average returns can create a misleading sense of security about a portfolio's chance of success, and its probability of success is doubtful. Notice that no specific details are included within this retirement wish. But as unreliable as betting on the long-term average is, it is still the most popular way I see people attempting to generate income from their investments.

Oftentimes, this flawed method of distribution is recommended by the very investment advisor that successfully helped the retiree save for retirement. I alluded to the fact in the previous chapter that the investment advisor who brought you to the dance isn't always the best person to take you home. Your investment advisor may have been an excellent coach in helping you build a retirement nest egg, but the methods and skill sets used to successfully accumulate retirement funds are vastly different from the skills necessary to properly distribute investment proceeds over a thirty-year retirement. If your current advisor doesn't create a goal-specific plan for you, or if they don't know how social security, Medicare, or pensions play into your retirement income plan, then you need to make a change.

I have been wearing glasses for thirty years. I finally broke down this past year and had LASIK surgery. Once the LASIK procedure was performed, the glasses that were once essential for me to function day to day for more than three decades were no longer useful. I threw them away. Just as my glasses were rendered useless when my situation changed, an investment professional that specializes in accumulating money for retirement may not be proficient in the proper distribution of those same funds during retirement. Find a retirement income specialist.

Wishing on a Product

Buying a product is not a substitute for having a goal-specific retirement income plan. Most individuals that recommend a product as a substitution for a plan are single-dimensional insurance salespeople, whose only desire is to sell an annuity—the only investment product they have to sell. We have already gone over the pitfalls of various types of annuities in previous chapters, so I won't belabor the problems with annuities. However, I do want to warn you one last time. Carefully study these products before you buy them. Make sure you really understand how these products work, and remember that all guarantees cost money—a surprising amount of money. The guarantees associated with these products are only as strong as the strength of the insurance company who issues them. Call me a skeptic, but I am highly doubtful that if there is a catastrophic collapse of our economic system and the greatest companies in the world such as Apple, Amazon, and ExxonMobil all become worthless, that the "Jack and Jill Insurance Company" of Coon Rapids, Iowa, will be there to guarantee your retirement savings.

The people who sell these products are not professionals that create and manage retirement income streams; they are commissioned salespeople. The questions of how much you will need and when will you need it will never be discussed. The features of their product, not your goals and plans, will be the topic of discussion. The purchase of an annuity, or, for that matter, any product, is not a viable substitute for a goal-based, detail-specific retirement income plan.

Wishing for Superior Investment Performance

Another group that tries to substitute a plan with a product is the group that I like to label as the "sophisticated underachievers," or those who attempt to achieve superior investment performance through market timing and superior investment selection. The product for sale in this instance is the superior investment prowess of whoever is managing the investment portfolio, whether it be your financial advisor, your mutual fund manager, or something or someone else. Please review Chapters 7 and 8 to help you remember why the dream of investment "exceptionalism" is simply that—a dream. Again, if there are no goals and no specifics on how to realize goals, you have a wish, not a plan.

2. THE RETIREMENT INCOME PLAN MUST CREATE A FRAMEWORK FOR DISTRIBUTION

When it comes to distributing, there is a single question that needs answering. How much should I withdraw from my investments? This question must be figured out if you are going to have a sustainable income stream throughout retirement, and if you are going to be able to enjoy your retirement experience to the fullest.

A sustainable withdrawal rate is a function of two factors: when future dollars will be needed for income, and how those dollars are invested until they are needed. Adjustments in either the timing of withdrawals or how retirement funds are invested will effectively change how much can be withdrawn safely from investments over a retirement period.

Basing the withdrawal percentage on the volumes of research that address this topic, it is recommended that only about 4% of an investment portfolio be withdrawn annually, if your objective is to maintain the investment principal.

When it comes to withdrawals at retirement, I have noticed two types of personalities. The first trait is manifested in individuals I will call the "spenders." The spenders take the attitude that, "I have been saving all my life for retirement, and I am now retired, so I am going to spend whatever I want." Spenders consider themselves wealthy and entitled; wealthy because they suddenly have more money at their disposal than at any time in their lives, and entitled because they have been scrimping and saving for forty years for retirement, so now that they are retired, it's fine to spend their hard-earned money on whatever they desire. The problem is that, without a well-defined distribution framework, the spenders end up blowing through all their retirement savings in the first decade of a three-decade retirement.

I can't tell you how many retirements have been destroyed because there was never a specific plan implemented to monitor retirement expenditures. Expensive RVs, second homes, and bailing children out of financial hardships all contribute to the self-destruction of early retirement overspending. Certainly, every retiree should enjoy the good things of life, but these expenditures need to be measured, monitored, and managed within a disciplined framework that ensures the retiree does not overspend and that they will have the money necessary to provide for expenses throughout their respective retirements.

Many spenders rationalize their actions by thinking that their life expectancy will somehow not be as long as the norm, or, somehow, they won't be needing as much income in the later years of retirement as they need during the early years. The unfortunate truth is that spenders and their spouses have just as much likelihood of living to their life expectancy, and beyond, as those who don't spend excessively.

The second unfortunate reality is that an inflation-adjusted income will still be necessary in the later years of being retired. Granted, older retirees will likely not be spending as much on recreation and travel as younger retirees do, but they do end up spending more for health care. The inflation rate for health care is roughly double the average inflation rate, so instead of paying for cruises and airline tickets, older retirees spend their income on prescriptions and deductibles. The bottom line is that an inflation-adjusted stream of income will still be necessary in the later stages of retirement.

During the late 1990s, many spenders got into trouble because they didn't follow the 4% withdrawal guideline. Investors during this time had enjoyed a decade of tremendous growth in their 401(k)s. The stock market had just gone through the best decade in history. I ran into several retirees who had experienced double-digit returns annually on their investments for ten years. They concluded that they could retire in their early fifties, because they could perpetually withdraw 8–10% annually from their retirement funds. They thought they were set for life.

These premature retirees forgot, or chose to ignore, that equities don't always go up. Well, the bursting of the dot-com bubble, 9/11, and the worst decade for the stock market since the Great Depression followed the nineties. Unfortunately, the early retirees of this period were forced back to work, after they had depleted much of their retirement savings accounts.

The second trait is exhibited in a group of retirees we'll call the "savers." Savers, as you have already surmised, are the opposite of the spenders. They are afraid of spending any of their retirement funds at all. They understand that even though the number they see on their financial statements is often quite large, they know this money has got to last them the rest of their lives, "and besides, who knows what the future might bring?" Savers became wealthy because of their frugality. They might have been forced to be penny-pinchers during their working careers, because every dollar they earned was dedicated to raising a family. They had to worry about paying for groceries, car insurance, college, and weddings, and they accumulated retirement portfolios only through much sacrifice and dedication.

Once the savers retire, it is difficult for them to change their frugal ways. Even though they can easily afford some of the simple pleasures in life, such as traveling to visit children or going to a restaurant on occasion, they choose not to. They just can't bring themselves to spend any money at all. They end up living well below their privilege, well below the wonderful lifestyle they created for themselves as they diligently socked away dollars during their working careers.

Just as the spenders ruin their own retirement by spending too much too early, the savers ruin their retirement by living below their potential and by denying themselves many of the simple pleasures and opportunities of retirement. Ironically, both the spenders and the savers would greatly benefit from the same date-specific, dollar-specific retirement income plan, a plan that would outline how much money could and should be withdrawn from investment accounts and when.

Creating a dependable stream of income from your retirement funds must be coordinated with your mailbox money. Your distribution plan will need to incorporate when Social Security benefits should start, how pensions should be paid out, the impact of required minimum distributions at age 70½, and the impact that taxes will have on all distributions.

The distribution plan will also need to consider the economic impact that the death of a spouse will have on the family income stream. Certainly, Social Security benefits and possibly pension benefits will be reduced at the death of a spouse. A distribution plan with specifics will be a great source of comfort to a grieving spouse and will go a long way in assisting the retirees to distribute their life savings responsibly. Additionally, the retiree will be able to live and spend with confidence, knowing they have a plan in place to provide for future income needs.

3. THE RETIREMENT INCOME PLAN MUST CREATE A FRAMEWORK FOR INVESTING

In previous chapters, I have made the argument that individuals need to have low-volatility investments in retirement, such as bank deposits and bonds, to provide a safe haven to draw income from when the stock market takes its occasional dive. I have also suggested that all retirees need equities in their portfolios in order to keep up with the price of goods and services. If low-volatility, fixed-income investments as well as high-volatility, inflation-fighting equities are necessary, two questions remain:

- How much of my retirement nest egg should be invested into low-volatility, fixed-income investments versus into inflation-beating but volatile equities?
- How should I withdraw income from these varying investments within my portfolio?

As the stock market goes through its occasional (but expected) temper tantrums, fixed-income investments keep our money safe from the routine upheaval of equities. The problem with fixed-income investments is that they never have, and likely never will, protect our purchasing power from the ravages of inflation. The longer we allow our money to be invested into fixed-income investments, the more our purchasing power diminishes. In the short term, fixed-income investments can protect our purchasing power from a slide in equities. In the long term, fixed-income investments will always leave us exposed to inflation.

Throughout this book, I have reminded you that over time, equities have outperformed almost every other asset class, and are one of the few asset classes that have managed to stay ahead of inflation. We must

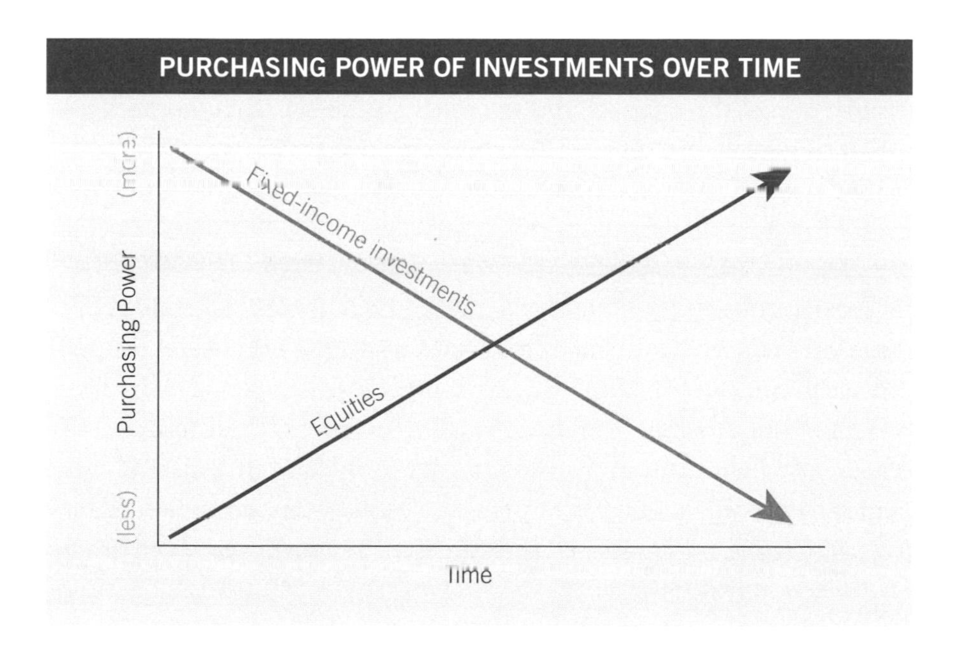

remember, however, that the price we have to pay to get inflation-beating returns is volatility. The shorter the period we have to invest, the more that stock market volatility will be a detriment to our investment success. Since 1925, money invested into large U.S. stocks, as represented by the S&P 500, and held for a decade or more have almost always given the investor a positive return. However, equities purchased and held for a single year lost money 26% of the years since 1925. In the short term, equities are temperamental, but over time, equities have always proven to be a great benefit.

So, if fixed-income investments are our short-term friends but long-term enemies, and equities can cause us problems in the short term but always reward us in the long term, it makes sense to come up with a program that takes advantage of the opposing nature of these two asset classes. Why wouldn't we invest the money we will need in the short-term into fixed-income type investments, and invest the money that we don't think we will need for a while into stock-related investments? This isn't rocket science here, folks. Of course, that's how we should invest. But most retirees don't invest this way. Why not?

I believe there are two reasons that most retirees fail to match their current investments with their future income needs.

First, the perceived value of most investment professionals is their ability to time the markets and to create a superior portfolio of investments. How would it go over with investors if their advisor were to tell them the truth? "Mr. and Mrs. Client, I really don't know what the markets will do next, and furthermore, I don't believe I can create a portfolio of investments that can outperform the stock market average." What a refreshing, honest statement that would be, but I don't expect you to hear that kind of candor any time soon. As we discussed previously, markets can't be timed, and "beating the markets" through superior investment selection is not a rational expectation. So, to answer the question—why don't we match our current investments to match our future income needs?—We don't invest this way because we allow our financial advisors (or possibly ourselves) to buy into the illusion that investment timing and selection will outperform the simple, yet powerful plan to allocate our investments, commensurate with when we will need to withdraw that money for our income needs.

Second, even if you agree with the methodology of allocating your short-term money to fixed income and your long-term money to equities, it is difficult to find a plan that you can follow to accomplish such a design. Most investment advisors adhere to the market-timing, stock-picking type of strategy, so a common-sense plan that accomplishes such an investment strategy is hard to find. Even if you are lucky enough to find such a plan, monitoring its progress is tedious at best.

The liberating truth is that a plan that allocates dollars we will need in the short term to fixed-income investments, and allocates dollars we will need in the long term to equities, frees us from the need to time the markets, or the need to outperform the stock market averages by superior investment selection. All we need is a date-specific, dollar-specific investment plan, the ability to monitor the plan, and then the discipline to follow such a plan.

4. THE RETIREMENT INCOME PLAN NEEDS TO CREATE A FRAMEWORK FOR REDUCING RISK

Retirees are particularly susceptible to three different kinds of risk:

1. Inflation risk
2. Stock market risk
3. Behavioral risk

A retirement income plan must recognize and minimize these risks whenever possible.

Inflation Risk

Remember, inflation is the gradual, but nonetheless lethal, loss of purchasing power. At just a 3% inflation rate, a dollar will only be able to purchase forty-one cents' worth of goods and services at the end of retirement. Unless you are willing to reduce your lifestyle and spending habits by about 60% during your retirement, inflation must be dealt with. Fortunately, the risk of inflation can be mitigated by how we invest.

Inflation risk is neutralized by investing into asset classes whose investment returns exceed the inflation rate. We beat inflation by investing into equities. Certainly, not all your retirement funds should be invested into equities, but some retirement assets need to be dedicated to beating inflation.

Stock Market Risk

If you are contemplating retirement, then you have been on the planet long enough to have experienced the occasional, very normal bouts of stock market volatility. The occasional market decline is part of the investment cycle. Successful investors understand declines and manage their finances accordingly; unsuccessful investors panic and turn temporary declines into permanent losses.

Stock market risk, or losing money by investing into equities, happens in only two possible ways. First, investors have a concentrated portfolio. In other words, the investor is not sufficiently diversified. If you buy stock in a single company, which then goes out of business, you'll lose money investing in stocks.

Quite simply, diversification is the way to mitigate this type of risk. The portfolios we manage consist of various ETFs and mutual funds that contain hundreds of different kinds of stocks. At the end of the day, our portfolios have ownership in large, medium, and small U.S. corporations, as well as a wide variety of foreign corporations. Individual companies can, and do, go out of business. Entire markets and economies, even though volatile at times, have proven to be incredibly resilient. They don't go away.

Second, investors lose money in the stock market when they choose to sell their equities at a lower price than they purchased them. In other words, investors who are diversified can only lose money when they choose to sell at the wrong time. No matter how unlucky you might be as an investor, leaving dollars invested over a prolonged period, in a diversified portfolio of equities, will eventually render positive results.

Successful investors in equities have the patience and discipline to wait out market corrections. They are not distracted by the short-term volatility that always accompanies investing in equities. Informed investors that are diversified don't lose money in the stock market. Their account balances certainly go down with everybody else's during bear markets, but because no selling takes place during these downturns, no money is lost. Unsuccessful investors, on the other hand, sell during down markets because they panic, and are punished for their impatience.

There has never been a time in the history of the stock market when a market decline was not eventually followed by a corresponding stock market increase, and the stock market eventually rose to a new record high. Never. Diversification, patience, and discipline are the essential ingredients that will reduce stock market risk. These attributes are rarely exhibited when goals, and plans to reach those goals, are absent.

Behavioral Risk

Legendary football coach Lou Holtz once said, "You don't need the big plays to win, you just have to eliminate the dumb ones." Likewise, anybody who knows anything about golf knows that it is not the player who gets the best shot of the day that wins the match; rather, it's the player who makes the fewest mistakes. The key is simple: just don't mess up!

Retirement is not a time for investment experimentation. It's not the time to ignorantly follow the crowd, or to be talked into investing your life savings into something you don't fully understand. It's not a time to be tossed to and fro by every headline you see on the nightly news or on the internet. Turning a working career's worth of accumulation into an income stream that will last the balance of your life takes thoughtful, deliberate planning. Of course, the investment products you choose to have your money invested into during retirement need to be tried-and-true products that have been thoroughly vetted and have withstood the test of time. You need to know why you are invested in these products, and when you will need to tap these particular investments for your future income needs. You need a date-specific, dollar-specific plan.

I didn't realize the behavioral impact of having an honest-to-goodness, goal-specific plan until the financial crisis of 2008–09. The retirement income plan I will introduce to you in the next several chapters was created in 2008, and was being implemented amongst my clientele in 2008–09. But when the financial crisis hit, only half of my clients had been converted to a formal plan.

I was shocked at what a difference having a goal-based plan was to my clients in the midst of the largest stock market decline of our lifetimes. As a reminder, the financial crisis of 2008–09 was a difficult time. Over the course of this crisis, the U.S. stock market plunged 57% and the international markets were likewise in turmoil. Many of the traditional "safe haven" products, where investors usually shelter money during market upheavals, were likewise losing money. Some of the largest and best financial institutions in the United States went out of business, and others were on the brink. The U.S. government was dumping unprecedented amounts of cash into the system to try to shore up the economy. Certainly, the investors of that time had never experienced anything like the crash of 2008–09, because there had been nothing akin to the events of this period since the Great Depression.

The negative news, compounded by the around-the-clock media coverage and commentary, had the investing public panicked. During this time, I was taking phone calls and meeting with all my clients. I noticed that the clients who didn't have a formal, date-specific, dollar-specific plan reacted very differently than those who had a plan.

Many of those without a formal plan were truly panicked. They saw the decline in their account balances, and sought to follow the conventional wisdom of that time by selling their investments and moving their money "someplace safe." Thankfully, my team and I were successful in convincing the vast majority of our investors of the wisdom of not selling in a panic at the bottom of the largest decline in our lifetimes. Unfortunately, some of our investors succumbed to the pressures. They sold and locked in their losses.

Remarkably, even though my clients who had adopted the goal-specific retirement income plans had investment returns very similar to those without formalized plans, they demonstrated much less anxiety, and were less prone to making investment errors based on the daily headlines. As I reviewed with these clients, I simply had to remind them of their plan, which, simply stated, was to take immediate income from non-stock or fixed-income investments, and not worry about the temporary and expected short-term volatility of their equities. Their plan was to have the inflation-fighting-equities part of their portfolio set aside to provide income in ten, fifteen, or even twenty years in the future. Short-term volatility in this part of the portfolio was expected and inconsequential.

The most commonly asked question back then was, "How long do you think this downturn will last?" I could show them that, historically speaking, the average bear market lasts only 15 months. Once the client understood that there was no need to liquidate their equities any time soon to provide themselves income, and that their goal-based plan took into consideration the occasional market slide, their fears diminished, and peace of mind was restored.

As with every bear market, 2008–09 was followed by a raging bull market. At the time of printing this book, the stock market has surged more than 300% since those dark days of the financial crisis. But, as certain as I am that bulls always follow bears, I am equally certain the next stock market upheaval is lurking in our future. Bear and bull markets can't be accurately forecasted, but they can surely be managed. A goal-specific income plan goes a long way toward helping to navigate the emotional roller coaster of investment management. A date-specific, dollar-specific retirement income plan helps to protect your future from perhaps its greatest threat—you.

CHAPTER 16

The Genesis of the Retirement Income Plan

"If your financial house is in order, you can afford to be patient."

—Robert Bishop

As an investment advisor to retirees, and as a lifelong student of retirement methods and practices, I enjoy reading white papers and professional journals regarding my favorite topic: managing money during retirement. I know what you are thinking. My family *also* thinks that there must be something wrong with me!

In 2007, I came across a paper[1] written by William Sharpe, a Nobel Prize-winning economist from Stanford, that I thought was particularly compelling.[2] In his paper, he suggests that when a person retires,

1. Sharpe, William F.; Scott, Jason S.; & Watson, John G. "Efficient Retirement Financial Strategies," July 2007.

2. I don't know if the concept of time segmentation was original to Sharpe. Since investigating time-segmented investing in greater depth, I have found others who have adopted similar patterns of investment management.

the retiree's investment funds would be divided into thirty separate accounts. Each of these accounts would be responsible for providing income for one year of a projected thirty-year retirement. So, there would be an account dedicated to providing income for the first year of retirement, an account dedicated to the second year of retirement income, and so on, until thirty years' worth of retirement income would be covered.

The value for such an approach to investing is obvious. Money set aside to provide income in the first year of retirement needs to be invested differently than money that won't be needed for thirty years. As we have previously discussed, short-term money and long-term money have different risks and different objectives.

Money set aside in an account to provide income during the first year of retirement has to be absolutely safe, and absolutely stable. It can't be subject to market fluctuations. Neither fighting inflation nor getting a large investment return is a concern with account #1, because of the shortness of its duration. Safety and stability are paramount. First-year money should be held in an ultra-conservative investment that is not subject to volatility.

On the other end of the spectrum is account #30, or the money that is designated to provide income during the thirtieth year of retirement. The objective of this account is to keep up with the erosion of purchasing power, so the dollars within this account will have to be invested in inflation-fighting equities. Short-term volatility is expected, but irrelevant in this account. This money won't be needed for three decades, and, speaking collectively, equities have never lost value and have always beaten inflation over time.

The thirty separate accounts would therefore start as being very conservatively invested, and then would get progressively more aggressive, as the need for income from these accounts is pushed out over twenty and thirty years. By following this pattern of investing, the retiree's short-term risk of being forced to sell equities in a down market is dissolved and the long-term threat of inflation is managed.

Sharpe is recommending a time-segmented approach to investing. He is suggesting that retirees match today's investment allocation with their future income needs.

Not long after reading Sharpe's paper, I visited one of those Christmas tree farms where you cut down your own tree. At the tree farm, I walked by the saplings, then the two-foot-tall trees, then the various progressively larger pine trees, until I arrived at the group of trees that had been prepared for people to harvest that year. The smaller pine trees in their various stages of growth were there to provide future income for the Christmas tree farm. I realized that the process of segmenting today's investments to match future income needs is very similar to how this Christmas tree farm operated. The farm had implemented a time-segmented approach of its own, as it had planned years in advance for its future income needs.

Sharpe's paper was a revelation to me. In my opinion, his relatively simple and straightforward approach to investment management for the retiree beat all the "timing and selecting" methods used by the "sophisticated underachievers" of the investment profession.

But as much as I liked Sharpe's concept in theory, it wasn't practical to implement. I didn't want to create and manage thirty separate accounts for each of my retirees, and certainly my retired clients didn't want to watch thirty separate accounts. The hassle and expense of this endeavor would have rendered the academically brilliant idea of time segmenting retirement funds impossible.

As I investigated further into the idea of transforming this concept into a practical model of investment management, I realized that I needed to adjust the length of time for each account. Managing six accounts that provided income for a five-year segment of time, versus the original one-year time frame, was workable, and followed the original objective Sharpe expressed. I therefore ended up with accounts that covered the first five years of retirement, the second five years of retirement, and so on, until thirty years of retirement were covered with just six manageable investment portfolios. In my office, we call these five-year periods "segments."

Upon further investigation, my staff found that certain custodians[3] allowed for individual accounts to be compartmentalized into "sleeves," which would allow us to benefit from managing six different sleeves of investment portfolios within a single account. This eliminated the need to open six separate accounts to obtain the desired segmentation, which saved the client the fees, trading costs, and hassle associated with having money managed over multiple brokerage accounts. We are now able to manage all six segments of a retiree's investment portfolio within a single account.

Once all the wrinkles of transitioning an idea into a methodology were ironed out, we launched our trademarked version of time-segmentation named The Perennial Income Model®. I will share details with you in the next chapter about how we constructed this model. For now, I want to share what it does.

The Perennial Income Model gives retirees a goal-based platform upon which they can manage their investments. Specifically, the Perennial Income Model® provides:

1. a framework for the distribution of retirement funds
2. a framework for investment of retirement accounts
3. a framework to manage risk

The Perennial Income Model[4] does not guarantee a stream of income. It is not impervious to the occasional stock market downturn, and it doesn't even attempt to "beat the market" or to get the highest

3. A custodian is a financial institution that holds customers' investments for safekeeping. These investments are typically held in electronic form. Most custodians also offer other services such as account administration, transaction settlements, collection of dividends and interest payments, and tax reporting. Some well-known custodians are TD Ameritrade, Charles Schwab, and Fidelity Investments.

4. The Perennial Income Model was created to help the retiree to know how their retirement funds should be divided and invested, with the intent of producing an inflation-adjusted stream of income throughout retirement. It provides guidelines for investing and distributing retirement accounts, but its assumptions and estimates are not guaranteed. The underlying investment performance will determine the outcome of this or any other investment program.

investment return in the universe. Its focus is to get the return the retiree needs so he or she can realize his or her individualized investment goals.

The Perennial Income Model is designed to provide a predictable, measurable stream of inflation-adjusted income to the retiree, with the least amount of risk, when all risks are taken into consideration. It insulates the risk of short-term stock market volatility because income in the short-term doesn't come from equities. It has built-in, inflation-fighting components because the inflation-fighting equities are owned in the later segments of the model.

The Perennial Income Model can provide peace of mind to those who implement and follow it. It acts as a behavior modifier, and helps the retiree remain committed to their long-term investment plan through periods of market uncertainty. When retirees understand what investments they own, why they own them, and how those investments fit into their overall financial future, they are less prone to panic. The Perennial Income Model acts as the very antidote to panic that is so dangerous to the financial future of retirees.

CHAPTER 17

Plan Construction

"It is better to prepare than to predict."

—*Hank Brock*

My intent in writing this chapter is to demonstrate how a time-segmented investment program is created and how it works—I am going to show you how we put together the Perennial Income Model. However, in sharing the workings of the Perennial Income Model, I feel somewhat like the negligent adult that hands the keys to a new sports car and a case of beer to a 16-year-old boy and says, "Here you go, this is all you need!"

Even though you may be very adept at creating spreadsheets, or you're able to put together a plan following the pattern I have provided in this chapter, please don't think you are done. Quite the contrary; you have just begun. Those who create a spreadsheet, invest, and then *forget* about their investments, or *abandon* their plan, will not have a successful outcome. When investor discipline fails, the plan fails. The essential steps of monitoring and harvesting (covered in Chapter 18) a time-segmentation program are *really* where the rubber meets the road, not just in the creation of the plan.

I do not recommend that you attempt to create and manage your own time-segmented distribution plan. There is so much more to managing money during retirement than creating a spreadsheet. Having knowledge of investments, taxes, Social Security, pensions, estate planning, and finance are all essential to successful money management. Discipline, patience, and experience are attributes that are likewise important for the person who manages your money.

I believe that very few retirees have all the knowledge and experience necessary to successfully manage retirement assets. After thirty years of managing money for retirees, I still don't have all the independent knowledge necessary. I have, therefore, surrounded myself with a highly-educated staff—Certified Financial Planners, Certified Public Accountants, and other tax and legal professionals—who all work collaboratively, with the goal of taking care of our clients.

The goal of a time-segmented plan is to produce a reliable stream of inflation adjusted income with the least overall risk, with the money that is either available or necessary to provide a desired level of income.

It is important to remember that a time-segmented plan is designed for income creation, and should not be used for investment dollars you will not likely need to convert into income during your lifetime. Money that you are confident will be passed to children or charities at your death should be invested independently from the money used for income creation.

PRE-CONSTRUCTION CONSIDERATIONS

When you decide which of your investments will be designated for income creation, you will be forced to consider your various investments and likely have to do some rearranging.

Most retirees have investments held in accounts with various registrations. Some of their investments are IRAs, some are Roth IRAs, some are held in after-tax brokerage accounts, and some in annuities. All of these registrations are taxed differently, thus these accounts will need to be placed in the correct segment, and invested properly within that segment, to be able to provide the future income appertaining to that segment.

For example, if you are sixty-five and constructing a plan, you must consider that at age 70½, the IRS will penalize you if you don't take the required minimum distribution (RMD)[1] from your IRA. You therefore must include some of your IRA money into a segment that coincides with future RMD requirements.

Another consideration is that Roth IRAs grow tax-free, are not subject to RMD distribution rules, and can be passed onto heirs that will continue to enjoy their tax-free status. Wouldn't it then make sense to have Roth IRAs invested in segments that provide income toward the end of a retirement? Because, if the money ends up not being needed and passes to heirs upon death, the heirs will be able to continue to enjoy the benefits of tax-free growth. If the Roth IRAs will not be needed for income for twenty to twenty-five years, and possibly will be passed on to heirs, they should be invested into equities because you need to protect purchasing power on money that will not be used for a couple of decades.

There are several other considerations you can and should contemplate before deciding how your investments should be allocated within the different segments. It is beyond the scope of this book to delve into all the tax and legal variables that should be deliberated before organizing your investments within the various segments. I just want to point out that it is important to think through the tax and legal issues of your own investments before plugging them into a time-segmented plan.

THE SMART FAMILY

I would now like to introduce you to a family we are going to build a time-segmented distribution plan for. The Smarts are a hypothetical

---

1. RMD (required minimum distribution). The amount an owner of an IRA or qualified retirement plan is required to distribute by the IRS from their accounts by April 1 following the year they reach age 70.5.

family, but their situation is similar to the real families we plan for daily. Tony Smart a sixty-five-year-old software engineer, has been diligently saving for retirement throughout his long career. He has come to the point where he and his wife, Kathy, are ready to do something else with their lives. They are ready to retire.

Tony and Kathy are the same age; they actually went to high school together. They raised four children, who are financially independent. Tony has been the major breadwinner for the family, but Kathy went back to school after the kids were raised to finish her degree. Kathy is currently the principal at the local junior high (she is *really* ready to retire).

Tony will be sixty-six by the time he retires, and his Social Security benefit will be $2,700, monthly. Kathy likewise has accumulated credits toward Social Security, but taking a spousal benefit of 50% of Tony's benefit would still net her more than if she were to file for Social Security based on her own earnings history. Kathy's spousal Social Security benefit will be $1,350 per month. Kathy has been with the school district for ten years, which makes her eligible for a pension. She will receive a pension payment of $700 per month. She elected the joint and survivor pension option, which means Tony will continue to receive Kathy's pension payment should Kathy predecease Tony.

Together, they have accumulated $1,000,000 in their 401(k) and IRA accounts. They want to know how this million dollars should be invested in a time-segmented program, and how much income they could expect to receive from that sum of money. They feel that a program spanning thirty years should be sufficient, and they would really like to pass the full million-dollar balance to their children upon their deaths, if possible.

LET'S BUILD THIS THING!

For simplicity's sake, let's initially build a time-segmented distribution plan for the Smart family *without* incorporating Social Security or pension payments, so you can clearly see how the retirement funds will be invested and then distributed throughout retirement. I will then illustrate for you how a time-segmented distribution plan works when mailbox money *is* incorporated.

We will divide the million dollars they have accumulated for retirement into seven different investment accounts. The first six accounts are assigned to a segment, and each segment is responsible to provide income for a five-year span of the Smart family's retirement. The seventh account, or the legacy segment, is designed to provide money for Tony and Kathy's heirs. The spreadsheet on the next page illustrates the time-segmentation program being built for the Smart family.

Segment 1 will provide income for the first five years of retirement. It will be put into a conservative account that will systematically distribute $3,801 monthly to Tony and Kathy's checking account. Even though equity-related investments have provided better returns than fixed-income types of investments in the long run, the Smarts aren't dealing with the long run. They will be liquidating all the money in segment 1 within the first five years of retirement, and the Smarts just can't risk the possibility of having this short-term investment be affected by a stock market decline. This piece of their portfolio must be dependable and free from volatility. It is the money they will be immediately dependent upon for monthly income.

The time-segmented program that they are adopting recognizes this need for safety and stability, so it's invested conservatively. Therefore, we can assume that segment 1 only gets a mere 1% return[2] on the money invested into it. Of the $1,000,000 invested into the overall segmentation program, 22.25% of the million dollars, or $222,526, is invested in this segment. This money is invested in a variety of short-term bonds and other very conservative fixed-income investments, which are by their very nature impervious to large swings in value.

While the money in segment 1 is being distributed to the Smarts for the first five years of retirement, the balance of the million dollars is growing. Of this money, 21.92%, or $219,221, is allocated to segment 2.

2. This book was written when interest rates in the United States were hovering at all-time lows. Five years ago, it would have been illogical to assume the extremely low fixed-income rates that I have used in this example. In five years, these same low-interest rate projections are likely to also be illogical. The assumed growth rates of those segments that are heavily invested into fixed income (segments 1 and 2) will need to be adjusted to reflect current economic conditions.

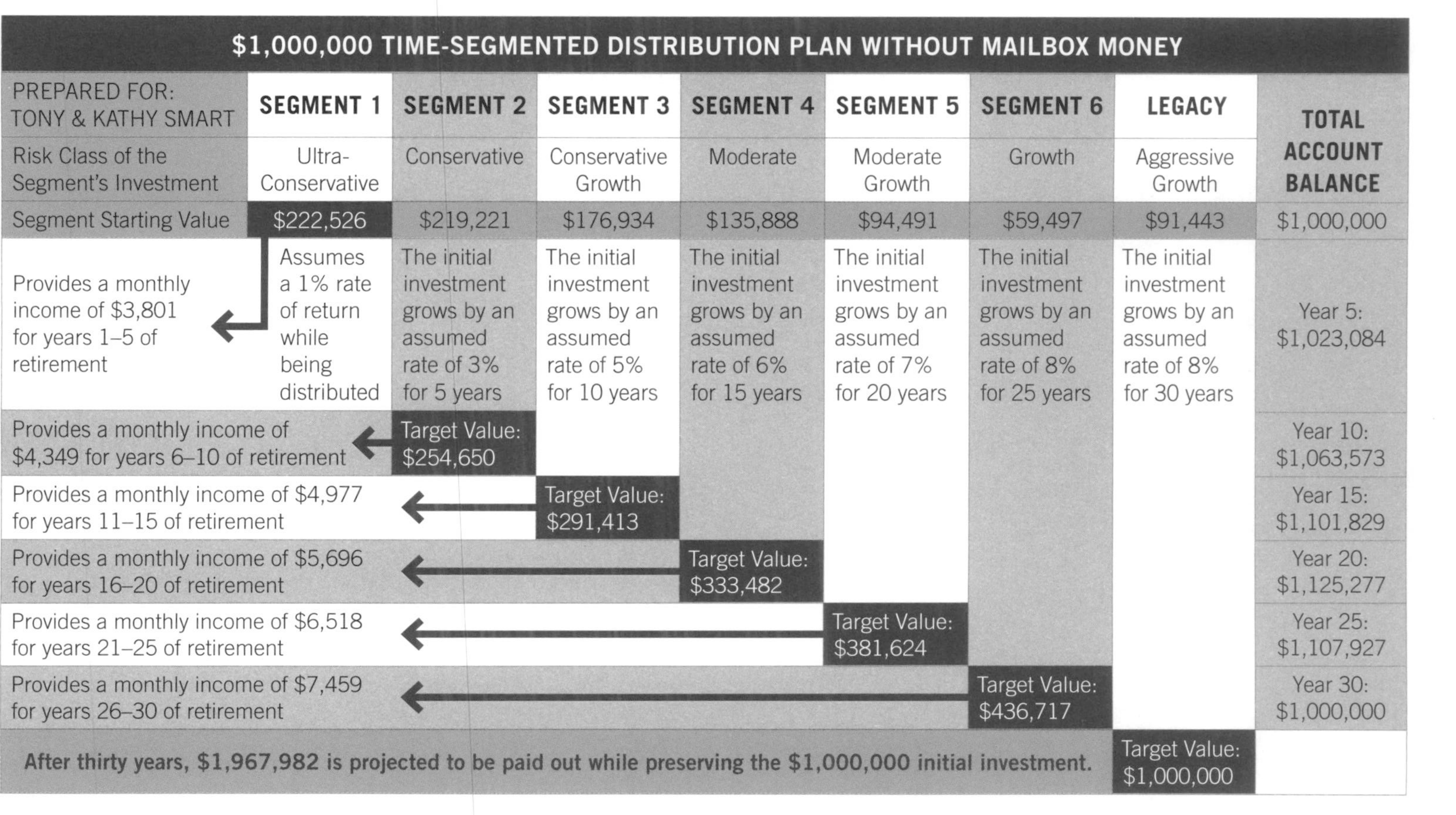

$1,000,000 TIME-SEGMENTED DISTRIBUTION PLAN WITHOUT MAILBOX MONEY

PREPARED FOR: TONY & KATHY SMART	SEGMENT 1	SEGMENT 2	SEGMENT 3	SEGMENT 4	SEGMENT 5	SEGMENT 6	LEGACY	TOTAL ACCOUNT BALANCE
Risk Class of the Segment's Investment	Ultra-Conservative	Conservative	Conservative Growth	Moderate	Moderate Growth	Growth	Aggressive Growth	
Segment Starting Value	$222,526	$219,221	$176,934	$135,888	$94,491	$59,497	$91,443	$1,000,000
Provides a monthly income of $3,801 for years 1–5 of retirement	Assumes a 1% rate of return while being distributed	The initial investment grows by an assumed rate of 3% for 5 years	The initial investment grows by an assumed rate of 5% for 10 years	The initial investment grows by an assumed rate of 6% for 15 years	The initial investment grows by an assumed rate of 7% for 20 years	The initial investment grows by an assumed rate of 8% for 25 years	The initial investment grows by an assumed rate of 8% for 30 years	Year 5: $1,023,084
Provides a monthly income of $4,349 for years 6–10 of retirement		Target Value: $254,650						Year 10: $1,063,573
Provides a monthly income of $4,977 for years 11–15 of retirement			Target Value: $291,413					Year 15: $1,101,829
Provides a monthly income of $5,696 for years 16–20 of retirement				Target Value: $333,482				Year 20: $1,125,277
Provides a monthly income of $6,518 for years 21–25 of retirement					Target Value: $381,624			Year 25: $1,107,927
Provides a monthly income of $7,459 for years 26–30 of retirement						Target Value: $436,717		Year 30: $1,000,000
After thirty years, $1,967,982 is projected to be paid out while preserving the $1,000,000 initial investment.							Target Value: $1,000,000	

The ideas presented above are for illustrative purposes only. Actual implementation and results will be different.

Segment 2 will take over the role of providing monthly income to Tony and Kathy once segment 1 runs out of money at the end of the fifth year. Since this money will not be needed for at least five years, it can be more aggressively invested than segment 1, but it can't be *significantly* more aggressive. A prolonged bear market could last longer than five years. Therefore, the bulk of this money should likewise avoid volatile investments. The time-segmented program assumes that the dollars sitting in segment 2 get a 3% return during the five years it is invested before being turned into income. If it were to get the assumed 3% rate of return, the original investment of $219,221 will have grown to the goal, or "target" value, of $245,650 by the beginning of the sixth year in preparation for distributing income for years six through ten. I have shaded the target values for each segment dark green.

Segment 3 is dedicated to providing income for the third five-year period of retirement, the years eleven through fifteen. Because this money is not necessary to provide income for ten years, this money can and should be more aggressively invested than segment 2. About half of this portfolio needs to be invested in equities, and the balance should be invested in less volatile fixed-income types of investments, such as bonds. Because of the moderate mix of investments within this segment, we will assume segment 3 will average a 5% growth rate. Segment 3 is given 17.64%, or $176,934, of the original million dollars. The goal of this segment is to average a 5%, annualized growth rate and to turn the original investment of $176,934 into the target amount of $291,413 by the time this segment is scheduled to provide income in year eleven.

Segment 4 is given 13.59%, or $135,888, of the original million dollars. Its goal is to turn the original investment of $135,888 into $333,482 by the time it's scheduled for producing income in year twenty of retirement. This goal will be realized if segment 4 gets a 6% annualized rate of return, so the bulk of this segment is invested into equities.

Segment 5 is given 9.45%, or $94,491, of the original million dollars and has twenty-five years to grow before it turns into income. The target amount of $381,624 will be realized if segment 5 averages 7% annually during the twenty years it is invested. Money in segment 5 covers income during years twenty-one through twenty-five. All of segment 5, as well as segment 6, must be invested into equities. These equities portfolios should be diversified, inexpensive, index-related investments that contain large, medium, and small U.S.-based stock companies, as well as international stocks from various sized companies and from a variety of regions and countries.

Segment 6 is given 5.95%, or $59,497, of the original million-dollar portfolio, and it will need to get a rate of return of 8% if it is to reach its target of $436,727 in year twenty-five. Segment 6 provides income for years twenty-five through thirty.

Segments 4, 5, and 6 are the inflation fighters. Segment 4 won't be used for income until the sixteenth year of retirement. There has never been a fifteen-year period in recorded history where the S&P 500 (or large U.S. stock) has not made money and beat inflation. Just as segment 1 had to be invested in fixed-income investments to fulfill its mission of providing stable income for the first five years of retirement, segments 4, 5, and 6 must be invested into equities in order to keep the Smart's investments ahead of inflation.

It is understood that these inflation-fighting segments will experience occasional bouts of volatility that the stock market imposes with regularity. The key to making the stock market work is to follow the segmentation plan, maintain discipline, and stay invested during times of volatility. With the time-segmented approach, there is no need to try to guess what the stock market will do next. Nobody can do that. You just have to be disciplined enough to stay invested. No matter what the pundits are saying, you can't ever give in and let yourself believe "the four most dangerous words in investing: 'This time it's different.'"[3] Certainly, every bear market is scary, but when the vast historical evidence is compiled, every bear market is remarkably similar. The stock market goes down about 30%, stays in negative territory for less than two years, and then the market recovers and goes on to eventual new highs.

3. Sir John Templeton, philanthropist and the founder of the Templeton Growth fund, was credited to have originated this phrase.

The greatest threat to the inflation-fighting segments 4, 5, and 6 is not getting caught in the next temporary decline in equities, but missing out on the next 300% bull market because you decided that it was a good time to get out of the markets. The decision to *not* sell one day will be the most important financial decision of your lifetime. This single decision may very well determine whether you maintain your independence and dignity during your lifetime or become dependent on others.

LEAVING A LEGACY

The last segment is what I like to call the legacy segment. Remember that Tony and Kathy wanted to leave their original $1,000,000 to their four children. If $91,443 of the original million dollars is invested in the legacy account, and that account gets an 8% rate of return, we can calculate that this $91,443 will grow to $1,000,000 in thirty years, the original amount the Smart family started with, at the beginning of their retirement.

During the later segments is where you can see the power of compound interest manifested. You can now see why Albert Einstein called compound interest the eighth wonder of the world, and the greatest power in the universe.

PLAN INSIGHTS

I just explained how a time-segmented program is created. Please refer to the spreadsheet on page 170 as I point out several important items:

First, the vertical column to the farthest right, the "Total Investment" column, shows the Smart family's projected total account balance. You might assume the overall account balance is going down as early segments are liquidated to provide income. But remember, as one segment is being liquidated, all the other segments are growing. This column gives you an idea of your overall account balance, or the actual money your heirs would receive, if you were to die in any given year and your investments got the assumed interest rate.

Second, the far left side of the spreadsheet illustrates the projected monthly income that would be derived from the investment portfolio. Notice that the monthly income starts at $3,801 but bumps up every fifth year. We developed the Perennial Income Model with inflation in mind. We have incorporated a 3% inflation adjustment into the income stream to account for expected erosion of purchasing power. We recognize that it will take more money to live in the future, and the Perennial Income Model is designed to provide you with a future higher income. Notice that over thirty years, $1,967,982 is projected to be paid out from the original $1,000,000, and the original $1,000,000 is projected to be intact after three decades of providing retirement income.

Third, notice that every segment is given an assumed growth rate. The assumptions we use in constructing the Perennial Income Model are merely educated guesses, and are not guarantees. I have come up with these assumptions through analyzing historical risks and returns of asset classes throughout the years, and I feel comfortable saying these assumed interest rates are realistic over a prolonged period. We assume only a 1% growth rate in segment 1, 3% for segment 2, and use growth assumptions of 5%, 6%, 7%, and 8% for segments 3–6. To put this all into perspective, the S&P 500 has averaged around 10% historically, and the largest assumed growth rate we use is in our most aggressive segment, is only 8%.

I believe it is a major mistake to assume growth rates that are unrealistically high, because nothing good is accomplished by making unrealistic growth assumptions. Certainly, the retiree might be pacified temporarily by projecting inflated growth assumptions, which would show larger incomes during retirement, but in the end, they are deceiving themselves and will be disappointed. When it comes to making growth assumptions, I suggest being a paranoid optimist. Plan for the worst and hope for the best. Surpluses are created when we under-project growth assumptions. Dealing with the management of surpluses versus deficits will make the retirement experience more secure and less stressful.

If you feel that my assumptions are overly aggressive, I invite you to use even more conservative assumptions in your own situation. No matter what assumptions you wish to use, the format of a time-segmented distribution plan can still be a valuable tool as you manage your retirement assets.

Fourth, you will see that every segment has a different "risk class" assigned to it. The risk class indicates how each segment should be invested. For example, Segment 4's risk class indicates that it should be moderately invested. Historically, moderately invested portfolios contain both equities and fixed-income investments, and have provided investment returns in the 6% range. Of course, every moderately managed investment will perform differently, so a vetting of investment products is always necessary.

You may have noted other aspects on the spreadsheet that are important. Notice that, because of compound interest, the money initially needed to be invested within each segment gets progressively smaller and more aggressively invested. Of course, every Perennial Income Model we create is customized for the individual's situation, but typically, the ratio of equities to fixed income types of investments for the overall Perennial Income Model is 60% equities/40% fixed income.

MAILBOX MONEY INTEGRATION

Let's now plug Tony and Kathy's mailbox money into the plan so you can see how this stream of income works with the cash flow stemming from the Smart's investments.

In the chart on the next page, we have listed the Smart's mailbox money. I have projected Tony's and Kathy's Social Security amounts, as well as Kathy's pension. The column on the far right is the total estimated monthly income, which will be received from the monthly systematic payments to the Smart family. Please note that the Social Security payments are projected to rise with inflation. Social Security cost-of-living adjustments are granted annually, depending on the previous year's inflation rate, as measured by the consumer price index. Instead of trying to guess an annual cost-of-living adjustment, we have adjusted the Social Security payments by the annualized rate of 2.6% every fifth year. This is the average rate that Social Security has grown by since its inception. Kathy's pension payment of $700 does not have a cost-of-living adjustment and will always be $700, as long as either Kathy or Tony is alive.

MAILBOX MONEY				
	Tony's Social Security	Kathy's Spousal Benefit	Kathy's Pension	Combined Monthly Total of Mailbox Money
Retirement Years	Inflation-Adjusted	Inflation-Adjusted	Not Inflation-Adjusted	
1–5	$2,700	$1,350	$700	$4,750
6–10	$3,085	$1,542	$700	$5,327
11–15	$3,524	$1,762	$700	$5,986
16–20	$4,026	$2,013	$700	$6,740
21–25	$4,600	$2,300	$700	$7,600
26–30	$5,256	$2,628	$700	$8,583

The ideas presented above are for illustrative purposes only. Actual implementation and results will be different.

The "Distribution Plan for Tony & Kathy Smart with Mailbox Money" spreadsheet on the opposite page shows how a Perennial Income Model would look after incorporating the Smart's mailbox money into the equation. We have designed this plan to maximize the Smart's monthly income. You will notice that we have added two new columns to the spreadsheet: "Mailbox Money" and "Total Income." The investment income column, plus the mailbox money column, equals the total income column, or the projected total monthly income amount the Smart family will be living on.

Now the framework for administering the Smart's retirement funds is in place. The next step is to manage money within the various segments, with predetermined investment goals in mind. This is where current investments are matched with future investment goals. Having date-specific, dollar-specific investment goals as a guide helps to direct you toward successful investment outcomes, as long as you maintain discipline by adhering to the program, monitoring progress, and harvesting investments when you reach your goals.

$1,000,000 TIME-SEGMENTED DISTRIBUTION PLAN WITH MAILBOX MONEY

PREPARED FOR: TONY & KATHY SMART					SEGMENT 1	SEGMENT 2	SEGMENT 3	SEGMENT 4	SEGMENT 5	SEGMENT 6	LEGACY
Risk Class of the Segment Investment					Ultra-Conservative	Conservative	Conservative Growth	Moderate	Moderate Growth	Growth	Aggressive Growth
Segment Starting Value					$213,552	$215,857	$178,[illegible]19	$139,445	$98,594	$62,989	$91,443
Age	Retirement Years	Total Monthly Income	Monthly Mailbox Money	Monthly Investment Income	Assumes a 1% rate of return while being distributed	The initial investment grows by an assumed rate of 3% for 5 years	The initial investment grows by an assumed rate of 5% for 10 years	The initial investment grows by an assumed rate of 6% for 15 years	The initial investment grows by an assumed rate of 7% for 20 years	The initial investment grows by an assumed rate of 8% for 25 years	The initial investment grows by an assumed rate of 8% for 30 years
66–70	1–5	$8,397	$4,750	$3,647							
71–75	6–10	$9,610	$5,327	$4,283		Target Value: $250,743					
76–80	11–15	$10,997	$5,986	$5,011			Target value: $293,364				
81–85	16–20	$12,584	$6,740	$5,845				Target Value: $342,212			
86–90	21–25	$14,401	$7,600	$6,801					Target Value: $398,194		
91–95	26–30	$16,480	$8,583	$7,897						Target Value: $462,352	
											Target Value: $1,000,000

The ideas presented here are for illustrative purposes only. Actual implementation and results will be different.

CHAPTER 18

Monitoring and Harvesting

"When performance is measured, performance improves. When performance is measured and reported, the rate of improvement accelerates."

—Thomas S. Monson

Time-segmented investing is appealing because it's goal based. Retirees understand *why* they are invested, *when* they will need a specific portion of their investments to provide future income, and *how* their dollars will need to be invested to accomplish each segment's goals. When retirees know how long an investment has to grow before being turned into income, they can confidently invest in each segment with the objective of meeting future goals with the least amount of risk. Remember, the primary risks retirees face are manifested in the short term as market volatility and in the long term as the erosion of purchasing power.

A PLAN SUPPORTS DISCIPLINE

Most investors don't invest with a goal in mind. They invest into a selection of securities, without much thought as to what the specific goal of a particular investment selection might be. In the rare event that a goal is selected, seldom is there any kind of monitoring to measure the progress of the investment program toward reaching the goal. Without goals, and without monitoring of progress, investor discipline evaporates, and the investor's guide ends up being their own emotions, combined with the influence of the prevailing current events. Such a combination usually portends disastrous consequences.

During stock market downturns, participants of a time-segmented plan can be reassured that equities are not being liquidated at a loss to provide monthly income. Instead, their monthly income is derived from the sale of fixed-income securities that are only minimally impacted by a stock market downturn. The equities they own will have certainly declined in value, but are not targeted for liquidation until ten, fifteen, or even twenty years into the future. Historically, the average duration of a bear market is less than two years.

Just as a winter storm becomes only a minor inconvenience if we are prepared, stock market hiccups should also be expected events, and should not disrupt the lifestyle or income flow of a disciplined retiree with a plan. Peace of mind is the result for the retiree who knows their plan is designed to provide income, even when parts of their portfolios are suffering through occasional and expected stock market declines. An additional measure of peace is afforded to the retiree that understands the risk of inflation is also being addressed by simply following the goal-based time-segmentation plan.

MONITORING AND HARVESTING

At first glance, the time-segmentation model becomes more aggressively invested as the retiree ages and gets into the latter segments of the plan. Having eighty- and ninety-year-old retirees with all their money invested into long-term, aggressive equity portfolios doesn't make any sense at all.

Fortunately, that is not how the program works, if the time-segmentation plan is properly monitored and harvested. The processes of monitoring and harvesting are imperative to the success of a time-segmented distribution plan. Let's talk about exactly what monitoring and harvesting investments means.

MONITORING PROGRESS

Like any plan, if there is no monitoring of progress toward a goal, a time-segmented investment plan will remain a wish or a dream that will never be realized. You may be asking yourself, "In this date-specific, dollar-specific program of time-segmented income distribution, what dates and dollars should I be monitoring?"

Each of the segments has an initial dollar amount, which is invested specific to its designated segment. The dollars invested within each segment will have a future liquidation date, or a date when the money within each of the segments will be turned into a five-year stream of income. There is a goal or a "target" amount of money that each of the investments within the segments needs to grow to in order to be able to fulfill its role of providing five years' worth of future income.

The targets for each of the segments is found in the dark green boxes in the graph found on the next page. Segment 1 provides income on day one of the program, so the target amount for segment 1 is the original amount of money dedicated to that segment. Segment 2 has a starting investment amount of $219,221. Given the assumed interest rate of 3% for segment 2, the target amount of money that will be necessary for segment 2 to have grown to by the end of the fifth year is $254,650. This target amount will then be distributed for years six through ten of retirement. This same pattern is followed for all the segments. Therefore, the monitoring of each segment's progress toward reaching its target by the target date is imperative. As progress is monitored, adjustments in the investments can be made as needed.

One of the biggest challenges with the time-segmented distribution approach is the difficulty of monitoring all the different segments. The "do it yourselfers," or those who create their own spreadsheets and try to manage and monitor their own segmentation programs, are particularly challenged because there is a lot to keep track of. I have invested many thousands of dollars to have software solutions created to help us construct and track the progress of the Perennial Income Models we manage. This software makes it possible for us to simultaneously oversee many different time-segmentation programs.

HARVESTING TO PRESERVE GAINS

A fruit farmer toils throughout the year in his orchard, fertilizing, pruning, spraying, and irrigating his trees. All this work is done because the farmer knows that in the fall, in a very short window of time, the trees will produce delicious fruit. He knows he must gather the fruit when it's ripe and ready to be harvested. Harvesting the fruit too early or too late in the season will ruin the fruit.

But just because the fruit is ready to be harvested on only a select few days of the year doesn't mean the fruit needs to be eaten only during the harvest. There are many methods that are used to preserve the fruit once it is gathered. The fruit can be frozen, canned, bottled, or dried to preserve its flavor and nutritional value for the future. The means of preserving the fruit is not nearly as meaningful as harvesting the fruit when it becomes perfectly ripe.

Just as the farmer picks his fruit at the appropriate time so it can be preserved for a future day, retirees should harvest their investment gains and preserve them once the targets are achieved for each segment. Unnecessary risk is brought to the time-segmentation plan if it is not properly harvested when the investment has ripened, or, in other words, grown to its target amount.

Simply stated, the process of harvesting, in financial terms, is transferring riskier, more volatile investments into a conservative and less volatile portfolio once the target of each segment is reached.

As I previously mentioned, within the Perennial Income Model, we use conservative growth assumptions. We do this in hopes that the target for each segment is reached prior to the date it will be needed to provide income.

To give you an example of how harvesting works, I will refer to the "Distribution Plan for Tony & Kathy Smart" spreadsheet on page 170. In segment 5, the target or goal is $381,624. We know that the $94,491 initially invested into segment 5 will grow to that amount, as long as the underlying investments in this segment grow by their assumed annualized 7% rate of return for twenty years.

Because we know the money invested in segment 5 won't be needed for income for twenty years, this segment must be invested into equities.

With all the peaks and valleys equities experience, the S&P 500 has still managed to average an 11.17%[1] annualized return since 1950. We are assuming only a 7% growth rate for segment 5, so it would be entirely possible that segment 5 could grow by more than a 7% annualized average return. If this segment, invested in equities, were to average an annualized return of 9% (2% less than its average return since 1950) instead of the assumed 7%, the original investment amount of $94,491 would grow to the target amount of $381,624 in sixteen years and two months, rather than in the projected twentieth year. Once the target amount is reached, no matter what year that happens to occur, the investment needs to be harvested and preserved. In other words, the equities in the segment that has obtained its target goal must be traded for more stable and conservative investments.

Some may say that by harvesting, we are limiting the growth of the investments within the segment that has been harvested. That assertion is true; growth will be slowed, because the harvested portfolio will have been changed from volatile equities to stable, fixed-income investments. At the same time, however, short-term volatility within the segment is also greatly reduced by transferring from equities to fixed income.

At this point, it is important to remember that the objective of the time-segmented approach to managing retirement funds is not to get the highest possible investment return. The stated objective is to provide the most stable, inflation-adjusted stream of income for the retiree—a stream of income that will last throughout retirement.

1. From January 1950 to April 2017 with dividends reinvested.

A time-segmented approach to investment management during retirement is designed for the intellectually honest person who understands that they really don't know much of what so many in the investment industry claim to know. They don't know what the market will do tomorrow. They don't know which mutual fund or stock will double in value next year. And they don't even know what channel or newsletter will give them the best and most up-to-date stock market tips and insights.

But these supposedly knowledge-deficient investors are in pretty good company. The best investors of the past and present likewise have not claimed to know the future. In fact, the best investors in history have labeled attempts to even guess future events and stock prices as foolishness.

The common thread I have found with successful investors, past and present, is that they believe in the wonder of the American economy. Successful investors become owners of the most prosperous corporations the world has ever known, and then they have the patience and discipline to let these companies go to work for them. I have never met an investor who has expressed regret from buying a diversified portfolio of equities five, ten, or fifteen years in the past. The time-segmented model of investment management is merely the tool that helps the retiree organize their finances so they can be an active participant in the miracle of the U.S. economy.

Conclusion

In the introduction of this book, I mentioned the enduring nature of the bristlecone pine tree. The bristlecone pine thrives in an unimaginably hostile environment because its roots run deep—it is well grounded, thus making it impervious to the day-to-day conditions of its environment. Through the course of this book I have shared with you concepts that, if understood and followed, will keep you "deeply rooted."

You have been warned about the investment fiction. It has been explained to you what *really* determines the growth of an investment. The difference between volatility and risk has been defined and the need to own equities to combat inflation has been explained. Finally, I shared with you how a time-segmented retirement distribution plan is constructed and monitored. All in an effort to help you to create a well-grounded, all-seasons retirement income plan that, like the bristlecone pine, is not susceptible to the daily conditions of its environment.

Your retirement income plan should be goal based and should serve as a guide to your financial decision-making for the rest of your life. It should drive your investment decisions, your withdrawal decisions, and even influence your spending, including your gifting decisions. With a plan in place, you will be ready to ward off the tsunami of negativity, misinformation, and sheer nonsense that is so prevalent when the topic of investing comes up. I can't protect you from being exposed to this drivel, but I hope I have done something better—helped you to disengage from it. Certainly, the economy and the stock market will continue to have their ups and downs, but for those with a plan, short-term events become irrelevant. Having a plan puts your financial house in order, and once your financial house is in order, you are free to pursue your retirement dreams.

As you look at a picture of a sunset or a sunrise, it is impossible to delineate between the two. The picture could be a sunset or a sunrise; it's up to you to decide. Your retirement experience can likewise be viewed as a sunset or a sunrise. Will your picture be like the setting of the sun, the winding down of a life? Or will your retirement picture be like a sunrise, filled with hopes and dreams as you look forward to the opportunities of a new day? You will determine your own retirement picture.

It is my hope that you *plan on living* an abundant retirement. The abundance I speak of is not just measured by the amount of dollars you accumulate. I am referring to the life you will experience as you serve others, spend time with those you love, and devote your life to pursuits that are truly meaningful to you.

APPENDIX

Hiring an Advisor

Retirees should be looking for a financial advisor that specializes in creating and monitoring retirement income plans and that are adept in dealing with retirement issues. If your potential advisor has limited knowledge regarding Social Security, pensions or retirement distribution methodologies, they aren't going to do a good job managing your retirement. Once you locate a possible candidate you need to ask this individual some questions.

At first it may feel awkward asking an advisor to answer some of the following questions, but remember, it is important to establish trust with the person who will be handling the financial future of your family. If the advisor doesn't sufficiently answer the questions or if you feel like they are trying to circumvent any of the questions, move on to the next advisor. Here are some interview questions you should ask:

Tell me about your qualifications, your background, and your education.

Listen for experience and skills that could be used to create a retirement income plan. Beware of red flags, i.e., being new to the business, works only part time, or mostly works with young executives rather than retirees. Warning: do not be overly impressed with titles such as wealth manager, senior specialist, account executive, financial advisor, or vice president of investments. Such labels hint at specialties or expertise when the titles are concocted for purely marketing purposes and do not delineate any special knowledge or ability. However, a couple of titles such as certified financial planner (CFP) and chartered financial consultant (ChFC) do require passing stringent tests as well as require ongoing continuing education.

Tell me about your licenses and registrations and explain to me how you get paid.

You should be able to quickly find out if the person is a commission-based advisor (a broker or a registered representative) or a fee-based advisor (registered investment advisor), or both. A registered representative gets a commission from each product they sell and the commissions vary from product to product. A registered investment advisor (RIA) should be able to produce a form ADV, which outlines their fee schedule. I believe you will be best served by working with a fee based RIA because their compensation is not tied to the sale of a product, rather their compensation is based on a predefined fee schedule. Working with an RIA, or a fee based advisor, eliminates many of the conflict of interest issues that could potentially impact investment advice. The investment professional's business card will reveal a lot about how that individual is licensed and how they conduct business.

Have you been disciplined for any unlawful or unethical actions in your professional career?

Although this question needs to be asked during the interview, it should be verified prior to the appointment at www.finra.org and/or www.adviserinfo.sec.gov, depending on the investment advisor's investment registrations. Do not settle on an advisor with complaints or an extensive history of moving from firm to firm. There are too many good investment advisors in the industry to settle for an individual with a history of problems.

What should I expect you to be able to do for me?

A good advisor will say things such as evaluate risk tolerance, establish time horizons, select suitable investments, rebalance portfolios, and help you to formulate and stick to a retirement income plan. Many advisors provide an investment policy statement (IPS) that details individualized investment strategies they will follow, in addition to written financial plans. Some advisors may have elaborately written financial plans, but the plans are not worth much if plans do not have realistic assumptions regarding inflation rate, rates of return, etc. Additionally, the plans must be monitored and adjusted regularly.

Tell me about your staff. What do they do? And how many clients do you service?

This question helps you to know if the advisor tries to cut corners and do it all on their own, or if they have a well-run organization that can take care of the you when the advisor is away. If true retirement income planning and implementation is involved, it would be very difficult for one retirement income planner to service hundreds of clients.

If I were to become a client, explain to me the process we would go through to develop a plan.

Listen for clues—is the investment advisor getting to really know your situation, not just your investments? Issues such as family, housing, health, lifestyle, and other concerns must be discussed. Beware of the advisor that is selling a product as a substitute for an actual plan. If the topic of conversation is focused on a product versus your situation, find another advisor.

How do you describe the ideal client?

Ideally, the advisor would describe you. If they describe a high-flying, risk-taking young executive, they aren't for you. A good follow-up question to that is, "Do you have account minimums?" You don't want to be the largest account the investment manager takes care of because the advisor may not have the experience or expertise to handle a larger account. You likewise do not want to be the smallest account with the advisor because then you won't get the attention you deserve.

How often will we communicate, and how?

Listen to the investment advisor's answer and then let them know your expectations. Remember, the investment advisor works for you. Some retirees like quarterly face-to-face reviews, some only want annual reviews. Accessibility is the key; the investment advisor should be there when you feel you need them. Websites, newsletters, emails, client events, workshops, etc., should be part of an ongoing effort to keep you informed.

How would you invest my money?

The retiree looking for a professional to provide a retirement income plan is not looking for a market timer, stock picker, or 30 percent returns. They're looking for solid market returns and, most importantly, a plan that can be implemented to provide inflation-adjusted income. Be wary of those who try to convince you that they can time the market. or concoct index beating portfolios. Also, listen to see if the investment advisor moves in and out of different investments often. This usually produces a lot of unnecessary trading costs and has not shown to increase investment results.

Do you have a working relationship with other professionals? Who? And how closely do you work with them?

A financial advisor should be the quarterback of a retirement income team and should coordinate all activities regarding your retirement income. However, the financial advisor, (just as a quarterback) is not the whole team and needs to work closely with the other members of the team: CPA, attorney, etc.

Maximizing all the sources of retirement income does not happen in a vacuum; careful consideration with tax, legal, and other professionals as needed is imperative for a successful long-term outcome. It is impossible for an investment advisor to know all there is to know about every subject that may impact your retirement. An advisor that recognizes his own limitations and collaborates with other financial professionals, in your behalf, is the kind of advisor you should be in search of.

Glossary

401(k): A defined-contribution plan offered by an employer to employees, which allows employees to set aside tax-deferred income for retirement purposes, and in some cases employers will match their contribution. See also *Defined-Contribution Plan.*

Active Management: The practice of attempting to cause one's portfolio to return more than the benchmark index of that portfolio, either through superior stock selection or by becoming more or less fully invested.

Asset Allocation: The process of dividing investments among different kinds of assets, such as stocks, bonds, real estate and cash, to optimize the risk/reward tradeoff based on an individual's or institution's specific situation and goals.

Baby Boomer: A person born between 1946 and 1964.

Bear Market: A downturn of at least 20% or more in multiple indexes (Dow or S&P 500) is considered an entry into a bear market.

Bonds: A debt investment in which an investor loans money to an entity, typically a corporation or government in return for a promised interest rate and the return of principal after a defined period of time.

Bull Market: The term "bull market" is most often used in respect to a rising stock market, but really can be applied to anything that is traded, such as bonds, currencies, commodities, etc.

Certificate of Deposit: CD; short or medium term, FDIC insured debt instrument offered by banks. CDs offer higher rates of return than most comparable investments, in exchange for tying up invested money for the duration of the certificate's maturity. CDs are low risk, low return investments.

Certified Public Accountant or CPA: The title of qualified accountants in the United States who have passed the Uniform Certified Public Accountant Examination and have met additional state education and experience requirements for certification as a CPA.

CERTIFIED FINANCIAL PLANNER™ or CFP® certificant: The title refers to the certification owned and awarded by the Certified Financial Planner Board of Standards, Inc. The CFP designation is awarded to individuals who successfully complete the CFP Board's initial and ongoing certification requirements.

Chartered Financial Consultant or ChFC®: A professional designation representing completion of a comprehensive course consisting of financial education, examinations and practical experience.

Commodities: Basic goods used in commerce that are interchangeable with other commodities of the same type. Examples include raw materials such as copper, oil, or soybeans.

Cost of Living Adjustment: COLA; an annual adjustment in Social Security to offset a change (usually a loss) in purchasing power, as measured by the Consumer Price Index.

Compound interest: Interest calculated on the initial principal and also on the accumulated interest. Also known as earning interest on interest.

Consumer Price Index: CPI; an inflationary indicator that measures the change in the cost of products and services, including housing, electricity, food, and transportation. The CPI is published monthly and is also known as the cost-of-living index.

Contract Value: The actual value of an annuity contract.

Correlation: A concept of diversification; using assets in a portfolio that move independently of each other, so when one goes down, the other stays the same or goes up. Assets which often move in opposite directions are negatively correlated. Having a negatively correlated and low correlated portfolio helps prevent losses in all sectors of a portfolio at the same time.

Custodian: A financial institution that holds customers' investments for safekeeping. These investments are typically held in electronic form. Most custodians also offer other services such as account administration, transaction settlements, collection of dividends and interest payments, and tax reporting.

Death Benefit Guarantee: A minimum guaranteed amount of money that will be paid to the beneficiary of an annuity, upon the death of the owner of the annuity.

Defined-Benefit Plan: A company retirement plan, such as a pension plan, in which a retired employee receives a specific monthly income based on salary history and years of service, and in which the employer bears the investment risk.

Defined-Contribution Plan: A company retirement plan, such as a 401(k) plan, in which the employee elects to defer some amount of his salary into the plan and bears the investment risk and the employers can match it.

Diversification: A portfolio strategy designed to reduce exposure to risk by combining a variety of investments, such as stocks, bonds, and real estate, which are unlikely to all move in the same direction. Therefore, the benefits of diversification will hold only if the securities in the portfolio are not perfectly correlated. The goal of diversification is to reduce the risk in a portfolio.

Employee Retirement Income Security Act of 1974: ERISA; the federal law which established legal guidelines for pension plan administration and investment practices.

Equities: Stocks or any other security ie: mutual funds and ETFs representing an ownership interest.

Estate Plan: Written document setting out an estate owner's instructions for disposition and administration of his or her property at his or her death, incapacity, or total disability.

Equity-Indexed Annuity: A class of annuity that returns are based on a specified equity-based index such as the S&P 500. Even though the returns are tied to a specific equity index, rate caps imposed by these products severely limit the potential for these products to realize a long-term results close to the indexes that these products are tied to. For example, if the S&P 500 were to surge 10, 15, or even 20 percent in a given year, the most an index annuity would credit is the cap rate. At the time this book was written, the prevailing cap rates were 4–5%.

In years when the stock index declines, index annuities typically guarantee a minimum return such as 2%.

Index annuities have large penalties if the annuity owner decides to liquidate their annuity before the end of the surrender period which typically last five to ten years.

Exchange-Traded Funds: ETF; a diversified investment vehicle similar to a mutual fund that mimics an index. ETFs trade like a stock on an exchange, thus experiencing price changes throughout the day as they are bought and sold anytime during market hours.

Expense Ratio: A measurement of the annual fees that all mutual funds or ETF's charge their shareholders. Expense Ratio expresses the percentage of assets deducted each fiscal year for fund expenses, including 12b-1 fees, management fees, administrative fees, operating costs, and all other asset-based costs incurred by the fund. Transaction costs incurred in the day to day operation of mutual funds and ETF's are not included in the expense ratio.

Financial Industry Regulatory Authority: FINRA; is an independent, non-governmental regulator for all securities firms doing business with the public in the United States. It is a self-regulatory organization responsible for the operation and regulation of the Nasdaq stock market and over-the-counter markets. FINRA investigates complaints against member firms and tries to ensure that all of its members adhere to both its own standards and those laid out by the Securities and Exchange Commission.

Financial Media: The content produced by journalists and news organizations covering financial topics. This content is often biased and used as a tool to sell or promote an idea or a product rather than providing credible financial information.

Fixed Annuity: An investment vehicle offered by an insurance company, that guarantees a stream of fixed payments over the life of the annuity. The insurer, not the insured, takes the investment risk.

Full Retirement Age: The age set forth in a retirement plan and for Social Security for employees to receive full benefits upon retirement. Retirement before the normal retirement age will result in a permanent reduction in benefits. For retirement age is age 66–67 depending on the year you were born.

Gross Domestic Product (GDP): A measure of the total value of all goods and services produced within a country during a year. GDP is commonly used as an indicator of the economic health of a country.

Harvesting Strategy: The act of liquidating investments once they have reached their goals to lock in the gains. This strategy is used in a time-segmented distribution plan. The liquidated assets are then put into safer investments until they are due to be used to create income. This limits gains in excess of the goal amount, but reduces risk from that segment of a retirement portfolio.

Industrial Revolution: Period marking the introduction of mass production, improved transportation, technological progress, and the industrial factory system. In the United States this period is generally agreed to have begun at the time of the Civil War (1861–1865) and continued into the next century.

Inflation: The sustained increase in the general price of goods and services, as measured by some broad index number of prices (such as Consumer Price Index) over months or years, and mirrored in the correspondingly decreasing purchasing power of the currency.

Investment Portfolio: A collection of two or more investments managed for a specific purpose.

IRA: Tax-deferred retirement plans that can be started by anyone who earns employment income or who is married to someone who earns employment income. Individuals who earn less than a certain amount (or who do not participate in their employer's retirement plan) can generally deduct a part or all of their contribution to such plans from their taxable income. Money in an IRA grows taxed deferred.

Liquidity: The degree to which an asset or security can be convertible into cash. Liquidity is characterized by a high level of trading activity. The stock of a very large company or country would be more liquid than that of a very small one.

Longevity risk: The risk that the amount of money an individual saves for retirement might not be enough to sustain them, due to increased life expectancy.

Market Correction: A reversal of the prevailing upward trend in price movements for securities. The term is most often used to describe a decline after a period of rising prices. A correction is often considered beneficial for the long term health of the market, in that the prices had risen too quickly and the drop put them back to more realistic levels.

Market Index: An index that measures the value of a group of stocks or investments that belong to a pre-defined group. An example would be the S&P 500 index which measures the value of the 500 largest publicly traded corporations in the United States. Another example is the MSCI EAFE Index which measures the performance of the 21 major stock indexes outside of the United States and Canada.

Market Timing: Belief that one can predict future market directions and invests based on this belief; attempting to predict when it would be good to sell or buy before a market movement.

Medicare: A federal health insurance program that pays for certain health care expenses for people aged 65 or older. Enrolled individuals must pay deductibles and co-payments, but much of their medical costs are covered by the program. Medicare is divided into four parts: Part A covers hospital bills, Part B covers doctor bills, Part C provides the option to choose from a package of health care plans, and Part D covers prescriptions.

Medicare Supplemental Insurance: A supplement to Medicare; various private supplemental health insurance plans sold to Medicare beneficiaries in the United States that provide coverage for medical expenses not or only partially covered by Medicare.

Morningstar: is an organization that provides independent investment analysis of various types of securities.

Mutual Fund: An investment vehicle made up of a pool of funds from many investors and is professionally managed being invested in stocks, bonds, short-term money market instruments, and/or other securities. The mutual fund will have a fund manager that trades the pooled money on a regular basis. The net proceeds are distributed or reinvested. Proportional tax gains and losses are passed to the mutual fund owner annually.

Old Age, Survivors, and Disability Insurance: OASDI; the official name for Social Security.

Passive Investing: The creation and maintenance of a portfolio which, as closely as possible replicates it's bench mark index.

Pension Benefit Guaranty Corporation: PBGC; a federal corporation established in 1974 ERISA, which is designed to provide limited protection of the vested benefits of pension plan participants.

Pension: Post-retirement benefits that an employee might receive from some employers. A pension is essentially compensation received by the employee after he/she has retired. See also *Defined-Benefit Plan*

Pension Rollover: The transfer of the lump-sum value of an employer sponsored pension benefit to an IRA

Perennial Income Model®: A proprietary time segmented portfolio construction technique designed and used by Peterson Wealth Advisors with the intent of providing consistent income during retirement.

Purchasing power: The value of a currency expressed in terms of the amount of goods or services that one unit of the currency can buy.

Registered Representative: An individual who is licensed to sell securities and has the legal power of an agent, having passed the securities licensing exams and requirements. Registered Representatives transact business through broker dealers and are typically commission based advisors.

Registered Investment Advisor: RIA; A fee-based vs. commission investment advisor registered with the SEC; Securities Exchange Commission or the securities authorities.

Required Minimum Distribution (RMD): The annual amount an owner of an IRA or qualified retirement plan is required to distribute from their accounts by April 1 following the year they reach age 70½.

Retirement Income Plan: A financial plan tailored to the specific needs of the retiree; takes into account longevity and inflation and seeks to provide the necessary retirement income at the lowest possible risk.

RIA: Registered Investment Advisor is a firm that engages in the act of providing investment advice for a fee. RIA's are governed by the Investment Advisers Act of 1940 and are registered either with the Securities and Exchange Commission (SEC) or state securities authorities.

Risk: The chance of a long-term, irreversible decline in ones' wealth; also, the chance that one will be forced to sell an investment at a temporarily decreased price.

Risk Tolerance: An investor's ability to handle variations in the value of his portfolio.

Roth IRA: An individual retirement account that allows a person to set aside after-tax income each year. Funds within the account grow tax-free and can be withdrawn in retirement tax free if certain conditions are met.

Safety: The probability of maintaining the value of one's wealth.

Securities and Exchange Commission (SEC): The primary federal regulatory agency for the securities industry. The SEC's aim is to promote full disclosure and to protect investors against fraudulent and manipulative practices in the securities markets.

Social Security: The comprehensive federal program of benefits providing workers and their dependents with retirement income, disability income, and other payments. The Social security tax (FICA) is used to pay for the program.

S&P 500: The Standard & Poor's 500 Index is an index of 500 largest United States public companies and is seen as an indicator of the performance of the US Stock Market.

Spousal Benefit: A provision of Social Security that allows spouses to collect up to one half (50%) of their spouse's Social Security benefit if it is larger than their own.

Stock: A type of security that represents ownership in a corporation. A holder of shares of stock is a partial owner of that company.

Survivor Benefit: A provision of Social Security that provides the surviving spouse with the highest of two benefits: their own benefit, or their deceased spouse's benefit.

Time Horizon: The length of time a sum of money is expected to be invested.

Time-Segmented Distribution: An income distribution plan that provides a balanced combination of safe and risky investments to achieve long-term retirement goals. Money is harvested in segments that are allowed to grow for a certain period of time before being used for income. As the risk increases in the segments less money is allocated to those segments, but the riskier segments provide more interest opportunity. Each segment is set up to provide income for a certain number of years.

Variable Annuity: A life insurance annuity contract which provides future payments to the holder (the annuitant), usually at retirement, the size of which depends on the performance of the portfolio's securities.

Volatility: A statistical measure of the dispersion of returns for a given security or market index. Volatility is ofttimes confused with risk. Volatility is the advent of a temporary decline or surge in the price of an investment while risk refers to the chance of a permanent loss.

Withdrawal Rate: The annual percentage of dollars that are withdrawn from a retirement portfolio. Although 4 percent is the number that is often used as the optimum withdrawal rate, there are always dissenting opinions both higher and lower when it comes to determining the ideal withdrawal rate during retirement.